The Black Death and the
Transformation of the West

The Black Death
and the Transformation of the West

DAVID HERLIHY

*Edited and with an Introduction
by Samuel K. Cohn, Jr.*

*Harvard University Press
Cambridge, Massachusetts, and London, England   1997*

940. 1
HER

12.00

B+T

9/26/97

Library of Congress Cataloging-in-Publication Data
Herlihy, David.
The black death and the transformation of the west /
David Herlihy; edited and with an introduction
by Samuel K. Cohn, Jr.
p. cm.
Includes bibliographical references and index.
ISBN 0-674-07612-5 (cloth : alk. paper).
—ISBN 0-674-07613-3 (paper : alk. paper)
1. Black death—Europe. 2. Diseases and history.
3. Civilization, Medieval. 4. Renaissance—Europe.
I. Cohn, Samuel Kline. II. Title.
RC178.A1H47 1997
940.1'92—dc21 96-54637

Designed by Gwen Nefsky Frankfeldt

Contents

The Black Death and the
Transformation of the West

Introduction

David Herlihy crossed a chronologically critical divide after completing his book on medieval Pisa[1] and a series of essays on the agricultural history of the early and central Middle Ages.[2] In the early 1960s he embarked on an investigation of the social and economic history of late medieval and Renaissance Europe, taking the Black Death of 1348 and its aftermath as the center of his analysis. This new focus characterized the bulk of his historical forays for the rest of his life. No matter what the subject—the history of popular piety, the networks of political elites, the family, women, or technology—the Black Death of 1348 and its consequences were central to his interpretative frameworks. Hence we were fortunate to find in Herlihy's stacks of research notes, computer files, and essays three unpublished lectures delivered at the University of Maine in 1985. With characteristic lucidity and boldness, these essays establish more clearly than anywhere else in his writing Herlihy's belief in the critical importance of the Black Death for the development of Western Europe and the transition from medieval to modern "systems" of behavior.

The three essays are not simply recapitulations of previously stated positions or revisions of previous research. Instead, they show an engagement with new sources for interpreting the Black

Death and a marked change of mind in Herlihy's conceptualization of the plague and its effects on medieval societies.[3]

The essays also, of course, follow the main lines of his thinking. Already in his first work on late medieval and Renaissance Italy he characterized the Black Death of 1348 as "the great watershed" in medieval demographic and economic history.[4] He had begun to chisel away at the Malthusian approach then current in the historiography of the plague in France and England as it had been set by the authoritative works of Emmanuel Le Roy Ladurie and M. M. Postan.[5] Herlihy's analysis of Pistoia replaced mortality with fertility as the critical variable for understanding Europe's failure to recover from the plague for over a century after its outbreak: "The failure of the birth rate to respond to the stimulus of deaths, more even than deaths themselves, seems the root cause of the shocking population plunge of the fourteenth century."[6]

Nonetheless, in sharp contrast to the three texts of 1985, Herlihy's diagnosis of the plague circa 1965 was still enmeshed in the broad Malthusian framework set by historians of the early 1960s. In the early 1970s, moreover, the importance of Malthusian cycles had become more pronounced in his work. In a "spectral analysis" of burial and death records, Herlihy and his statistician colleagues drew a symbiotic relationship between cycles of fertility and mortality in which the peaks in mortality were driven by fertility:

> The cycle of death rates, we propose, is closely related to, and in some sense may be considered in delayed reciprocal movement with, the cycle of birth rates. The high mortalities of a major plague stimulated the formation of a large age cohort, relative to the older population, in the following years, and this cohort was also likely to prepare another plague outbreak some forty or more years later, when it was most actively reproducing.[7]

True, Herlihy had eloquently demonstrated the shortcomings of a Malthusian model that stressed only the "positive" checks without any discussion of the "moral constraints," which Malthus emphasized in subsequent editions of *An Essay on the Principles of Population*.[8] By such a reckoning the plague should have struck much earlier—in Pistoia, even before the recurrence of famines in the early fourteenth century and possibly as early as the mid-thirteenth century. Moreover, a crude Malthusian model was inadequate for explaining the delay of European populations to recover their losses during the fifteenth century. Yet in Herlihy's work on Pistoia it was the social, political, and economic conditions—overpopulation, over-extended planting of wheat, burdensome taxes in the countryside heaped on those least able to pay, and poor living standards for the mass of the population—that formed the crucible from which pestilence, even if delayed, would emerge by the mid-fourteenth century to change the ecology of Europe.

In both his article of 1965 and his book on Pistoia Herlihy concluded his discussion of the plague by turning to the account of the contemporary chronicler of Florence, Giovanni Villani, himself struck down by the pestilence of 1348. In his last days Villani had asked whether the disasters of his day should be attributed to factors beyond human responsibility—blind chance or the forces set in motion by celestial conjunctions—or whether they were to be interpreted as divine retribution for the present-day sins of the Florentines—"avarice, greed and usurious oppression of the poor."[9] Like Villani, Herlihy in the 1960s chose the second explanation, which he rendered into modern terms as man-made social factors to explain the plague's devastation of Europe.[10]

By 1985 Herlihy had changed his mind. Had he chosen to return to Villani's interpretive dilemma, he would have picked the first of the Florentine chronicler's explanations. For Herlihy's analysis, the plague now had little if anything to do with social forces. He had moved away from his modified Malthusian framework of the 1960s, in which his stress on the role of class and exploitation of the countryside might even be seen as an unstated Marxist perspective (though Herlihy would have denied this interpretation). By the 1980s he no longer saw late medieval society headed inexorably towards a Malthusian disaster; instead, he saw it locked in a "stalemate" or "deadlock." The plague was not historically necessary, and without it Europe may have well persisted with remarkably stable institutions and systems of behavior for millennia. By his later interpretation, the Black Death had become an external factor independent of the social, political, or even the demographic environment. Once it had struck, however, it set Europe on a new path almost totally unrelated to its late medieval social past.[11]

Why had Herlihy changed his mind? Part of the explanation might be traced to a conference of 1983, during which the Italian demographer Massimo Livi-Bacci, among others, had argued vigorously against any causal link between malnutrition and plague or, for that matter, between malnutrition and many other epidemic diseases. Indeed, it would appear that malnutrition often served as a prophylactic against disease.[12] In addition, as Herlihy's first essay attests, he was swayed by Bruce Campbell's study of the Norfolk village of Coltishall, in which Campbell argued that even the famines of 1314–1317 did not alter the "demographic status quo," that the plague "was the result not of economic but of biological factors," and that it was "an exogamous variable."[13]

But what was even more crucial to Herlihy's change of mind in interpreting the distant past was the emergence in our own times of the pestilence we have called AIDS. Indeed, Herlihy opens these essays on the Black Death by pointing to the cholera epidemic of the 1820s as the stimulus for modern historiographical interest in the late medieval plagues. He further claims that society's preoccupation with our own current pestilence similarly has stimulated a renewed interest in the Black Death.[14]

But the rapid dissemination of AIDS, unlike that of typhus,[15] cholera,[16] or tuberculosis later in the nineteenth century,[17] cannot be pinned on social conditions that may have arisen from urbanization, industrialization, or inequalities in class structure. The origins of AIDS, as with the plague of 1348, remain more mysterious. AIDS too appears to have arisen ex-nihilo and—despite the propaganda of religious and homophobic commentators— looks to us, as the plague of 1348 did to the people of medieval Europe, like an inexplicable and horrific exogamous calamity.[18]

While the etiology and spread of syphilis in the sixteenth century would certainly make a better historical parallel to the present AIDS epidemic than does the Black Death,[19] Herlihy draws parallels from the Black Death experience of the later Middle Ages to our present-day predicament. These parallels lie largely in the history of attitudes. Perhaps stemming from the utter mystery of these two epidemics in contrast to syphilis in the sixteenth, cholera in the nineteenth, and tuberculosis in the late nineteenth and twentieth centuries[20]—all highly contagious diseases—AIDS and the Black Death heightened popular distrust of expert opinion, particularly of the medical profession,[21] and have led more forcefully to suspicions, fears, and hatreds of the alien.[22] In the fourteenth century the plague gave rise to the spread of anti-Semitism—the rumor and persecution of Jews as poisoners of wells[23]; today it has reinvigorated fears and hatred of homosexuals and the poor. These suggestions surely invite some closer comparative studies of the outbreak of new diseases through modern history, all of which to a greater or lesser extent have sought out scapegoats for blame and had beginnings that were clouded in mystery in both the medical and lay communities.[24]

Finally, the AIDS epidemic may well have inspired Herlihy's skepticism about the methods commonly used since the late nineteenth century of analyzing the fourteenth- and fifteenth-century plagues. The rapid mutations of viruses and the appearance of new ones without any known historical precedents should cause us to be wary of any match between diseases of the past and those that have been clinically described since the end of the nineteenth century. While bacteriologists and zoologists have recently questioned whether the bubonic plague was the only or even the principal disease in 1348 and in subsequent strikes of high mortality during the later Middle Ages,[25] the attempt to match medieval plague descriptions with modern diseases may be wrongheaded, even if the reports of medieval chroniclers and physicians can be trusted and deciphered in clinical terms. Modern medicine and the rapid dissemination of AIDS have taught the layman that new diseases can emerge in history without precise precedents, and that, perhaps as mysteriously as they appeared, they can vanish from the pool of infectious diseases. Thus medieval chronicles and doctors may not have been so blind or foolish in failing to discover the rat-flea nexus as twentieth-century historians have often assumed. As Herlihy concludes from what contemporary chroniclers, story-tellers, and doctors said, as well as from what they did not report, this failure to notice the rat-flea relation of *Yersinia pestis* may be justified by the simple fact that the connection did not exist.[26]

In these essays, as in Herlihy's historical writing more generally, the reader will find no trace of any lackluster recounting of the old historical debates. Instead, the author engages afresh with new sources as he continues to depend on the old ones in formulating new ideas. Like a finely tuned detective story, the first chapter marshals evidence to claim that the Black Death of 1348 was most likely not the bubonic plague assumed by historians since the late nineteenth century.[27] Instead, Herlihy takes seriously the thesis of the zoologist Graham Twigg, largely ignored or dismissed as nonhistorical by the rest of the historical profession, who has shown that the plagues in late medieval Britain could not possibly have been either pneumonic or bubonic.[28] While not completely agreeing with Twigg's solution—that the epidemic of 1348–49 was the spread of anthrax—Herlihy expands Twigg's argument against the bubonic plague in Great Britain to Europe more generally, emphasizing the complete absence of any contemporary evidence of a preceding epizootic among rodents.

Ingeniously, Herlihy reaches for another source of evidence heretofore untapped by the historians of epidemics—the acts and processes for conferring sainthood, later collected in abbreviated form in the *Acta Sanctorum*. From these, he discovers that the late fourteenth- and fifteenth-century laity sought out new spiritual patrons for protection against the plague, reaching back to obscure figures such as the thirteenth-century Rose of Viterbo, about whom stories of miracle cures for the later pestilence were invented. In these accounts, similar to the descriptions by the most authoritative doctor of the period, Guy de Chauliac, Pope Clement VI's physician at Avignon, Herlihy finds that the buboes characteristic of (though not unique to) the bubonic plague were not the thing commonly described as "the sign" of plague; instead, these sources refer to *lenticulae* or freckles, which were more common to a number of other diseases including anthrax.[29]

The subsequent two chapters turn to the consequences of the plague for European civilization writ large: first, the demographic and economic consequences; second, those for the history of cultural attitudes. Again, Herlihy emphasizes that the decisive transition in the late fourteenth century from medieval to modern "systems of behavior" was not inevitable but depended directly on that most grand and horrific of external variables, the Black Death of 1348 and subsequent strikes of the disease against European populations through the early fifteenth century. From these, Herlihy creates two models of change: one regards the economic "system," the other, the demographic. In the economic sphere,

Herlihy sees in the Black Death the mother of technological advance as societies strove to create labor-saving devices in the wake of population depletion. In the demographic system, he finds a shift in population control from "positive checks," such as disease, war, and famine, to a post-plague demography controlled principally by "preventive checks," that is, controls that stemmed from changes in inheritance practices, ages at marriage, and even birth control. Taking the place of strikes of high mortality, these "preventive" checks would come to distinguish Britain by the seventeenth century,[30] and perhaps also other areas of Europe yet to be systematically studied through the early modern period.

The final chapter turns to culture. Eschewing the debates founded on such classic works as Huizinga's *The Waning of the Middle Ages,*[31] Millard Meiss's *Painting in Florence and Siena after the Black Death,*[32] Alberto Tenenti's *Il senso della morte,*[33] and Philippe Ariès's *The Hour of Our Death,*[34] Herlihy turns to a new type of evidence, the rise in the frequency of Christian first names given to newborns, to propose an intriguing hypothesis: the plague's role in the spread of Christianity as a part of popular culture. Moreover, he gives new clarity and force to older themes such as the role of plague in the dissemination of vernacular cultures and the rise of proto-nationalist urges; he does not simply enumerate these as effects of the plague by virtue of coming afterwards.[35]

Herlihy's novel and bold conceptualizations will inspire students and professional historians alike to rethink the plague along his broad lines of interpretation: to refine or perhaps even to refute altogether some of his sweeping generalizations. In regard to the post-plague demographic system in which families limited the number of offspring to achieve or maintain greater prosperity, an additional idea is suggested by his argument: with the Black Death and its tragic onslaught, which by many accounts struck down a disproportionate number of the young, a new, more cherishing view of children arose during the late fourteenth and fifteenth centuries. As with many of the plague's reactions, its long- and short-term consequences were often mirror opposites of one another. In the face of the 1348 unprecedented disaster, fathers and mothers may well have abandoned their children, as one contemporary chronicler or story-teller after another reported and repeated. "Oh father, why have you abandoned me? . . . Mother, where have you gone?" were among the laments recorded by the 1348 chronicler from Piacenza, Gabrielle de' Mussis.[36] Boccaccio ended his lament over relatives abandoning one another by reporting that "what is hardly believable, fathers and mothers [abandoned] their children as though they were not their own, disgusted by seeing or assisting them."[37] Yet by the time of the later onslaughts of pestilence in the fourteenth and fifteenth centuries, familial sentiments had radically shifted. Here, the complaints of the post-plague William Langland might be compared with those of the pre-plague Sienese poet Cecco Angiolieri. Disinherited from his worldly possessions because of the selfish pietistic zeal of his parents, Cecco penned his famous ode of familial hatred:

> If I were death I would go to my father;
> If I were life I would flee from him;
> And I would do the same for my mother.[38]

In contrast, a century later, Langland criticized parents of the merchant classes for spoiling their children, and suggested that the plague and rampant mortality may have been the cause of their parental overindulgence:

> Don't let wealth spoil them while they are young
> Nor for fear of the pestilence indulge them beyond reason.[39]

Beyond these literary impressions, the historian might turn to a more systematic source—last wills and testaments—which at least for central and northern Italy included large swathes of rural and urban populations as early as the last decades of the thirteenth century.[40] In samples from Tuscany and Umbria, testaments show a steady progression in the importance of children. Men and women alike whittled down long lists of itemized gifts for numerous pious as well as nonpious causes to concentrate their attention on their surviving offspring as the universal heirs, spelling out with increasing detail the terms of these final allocations. By the early sixteenth century, the bulk of last wills and testaments in central and northern Italy came to focus on surviving sons. In near-religious terms, the children (usually but not always the sons) were seen as the conduits and repositories for the continuation and preservation of familial blood lines, which came to mark a new sense of earthly immortality.[41]

As well as provoking ideas in sympathy with Herlihy's broad lines of argument, these essays will no doubt invite modifications and objections. Did the Black Death mark a fundamental change in medical theory, leading toward a new theory of contagion? Was the Black Death the central turning point in the history of technology in Western Europe? Did the Black Death and its onslaught on European populations in fact spur new labor-saving technology? In arguing that the plague set off a new wave of technological ingenuity that would lead inexorably to the Industrial Revolution, Herlihy points to labor-saving devices invented after the Black Death of 1348. One of the most provocative of his examples is Johann Gutenberg's printing press, invented in 1453. This, he suggests, came to replace the large teams of monastic copyists who, because of their cloistered life, may have been cut down more severely than the general population by the plague. But if the historian looks more closely at the period of the diffusion of this new technology instead of its date of invention, a different relationship between technology and population emerges. Although the printing press had been invented during the trough of European population in the mid-fifteenth century, the "takeoff" in the printing industry as marked by surviving publications *(incunabula)* did not occur until the 1470s—that is, when the population of Europe was no longer falling or even stagnant but was once again surging forward (see figure below). Moreover, the most important centers of printing—Venice, Rome, and the southern German cities and principalities—were not places of lagging population growth but instead were experiencing the fastest demographic growth in all of Europe.[42]

Nor was the immediate post-plague period or even the fifteenth century particularly noted for technological advances in other sectors. For wool and silk manufacture, the major breakthroughs (before the Industrial Revolution) came earlier, indeed during the period of surplus labor in the late thirteenth and early fourteenth centuries.[43] The same might be said of agriculture.[44] While the agricultural depression of the fifteenth century may have led to some labor-saving devices such as a light one-stilt

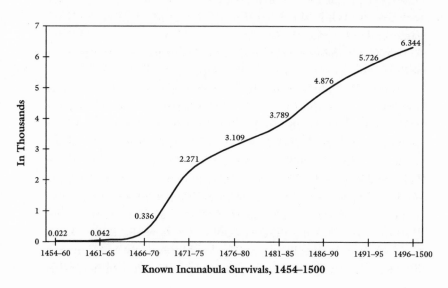

Known Incunabula Survivals, 1454–1500

plough, other agricultural practices—the expansion of complex field systems, the extensive planting of vetches, the Hainault scythe—had clearly antedated the plague, spreading through large parts of Europe in the early fourteenth century.[45] The diffusion of other technological innovations such as windmills, which the Crusaders brought to the West in the twelfth century, depended not on labor scarcity but on the great expansion of wheat production spawned by European demographic expansion of the late twelfth and thirteenth centuries.[46] For Norfolk, Bruce Campbell and Mark Overton have recently argued that before the agricultural revolution of the mid-eighteenth century, "all the technological innovations that brought it about can be found as far back as the thirteenth century." In their survey of six centuries of yield ratios, the Black Death and its aftermath were absolutely of no consequence to broad changes in Norfolk agriculture.[47]

Finally, despite the upsurge in warfare in France and Italy during the second half of the fourteenth and early fifteenth centuries, the plague did not mark widespread innovations in military technology. While the invention of the canon and gunpowder came earlier, in the thirteenth century,[48] the so-called Military Revolution came later, in the sixteenth century, and at a time of population increase and even overpopulation.[49]

Second, Herlihy's provocative analysis of Christian names as marking the spread of Christianity through the unlearned layers of Western society is also questionable, as indeed he later realized in one of his last publications.[50] While the absence of saints' names such as Giovanni, Antonio, Niccolò, and Francesco in the *Libro di Montaperti* (1260) is striking in comparison to their later predominance in the Florentine monastic necrologies of the fifteenth century and the Catasto of 1427, a closer look at the chronology of naming practices does not show the Black Death of 1348 as the watershed. As Charles Marie de la Roncière has shown, the change in the choice of names came earlier, with the spread of mendicant preaching through the countryside during the first half of the fourteenth century.[51] Indeed, the Black Death of 1348, at least in the short run, had the very opposite effect. The rural populations of the Florentine *contado* recoiled against the popular naming practices of the past several generations; instead of increasing, mendicant saints' names such as Francesco declined during the second half of the fourteenth century.[52]

Later, Herlihy even questioned whether the appearance of saints' names can be taken as evidence of Christianization, suggesting that they express instead psychological needs for protectors in the face of adversity. What exactly caused that adversity remains a mystery in Herlihy's account, since the change in naming practices came about fifty years before the advent of plague.[53] In his later essay, Herlihy stressed the reduction of the stock of personal names over his earlier emphasis on the change to saints' names. That, again, was a change that preceded the Black Death and that was spurred by a growth in both ecclesiastical and secular bureaucracies during the thirteenth century.[54]

Herlihy's sweeping analyses for Western Europe cry out for comparative investigations. Were the social, political, and psychological consequences of the Black Death as uniform throughout Western Europe as Herlihy's essays imply?[55] And how do we account for the sharp differences between eastern and western Europe in economic and social developments set off by the plague[56] or, even more profoundly, between the West and the Middle East, where the plague was as virulent if not more so than in the West?[57]

In the Moslem areas of the Mediterranean and Asia Minor, the plague appears to have set in motion a chain of reactions just opposite to that described by Herlihy and others for the West. As against the rapid dismemberment of regimes and scores of popular revolts in the West, Mamluk political control was unshaken by the plague experience. Further, far more than may have been the case in the West, commerce, industry, and agricultural productivity declined rapidly in the East after the plague and failed to recover during the fifteenth century. In the Moslem countries surveyed by Michael Dols, the decline of rural population in no way aided "the long-term improvement of agrarian technology or the re-allocation of resources" as, some have argued, it did in Western Europe.[58] Nor did the Black Death set off bitter factional rivalries in the East between Moslem neighbors or foster hatred of aliens and waves of anti-Semitic pogroms as it did in numerous localities throughout Western Europe. How do we explain these differences? Is it enough to point to the plague alone to understand these broad developments and differences in politics, economy, technology, and mentality between the East and the West?[59]

Finally, historians may draw different lessons from our contemporary experience with the AIDS epidemic and the eruptions and rapid mutations of new viruses at ever frightening rates from those evocatively proposed by Herlihy. Indeed, in contrast to Campbell's and Herlihy's utter skepticism about the relationship between societal conditions and the great mortalities set in course in 1348, future historians might emphasize once again the importance of the underlying social conditions. In parallel with Marc Bloch's interpretation of the plague as a "psychological fact" and the development of late medieval trade as the necessary precondition for the plague's dissemination over Europe,[60] they might draw on recent epidemiology and the explanation of the diffusion of new viruses over the past decade as the result of certain societal factors—rapid global migration and mass travel—that have paved the way for the new "superhighways" of viral infections.[61]

No doubt the courageous interpretations and creative syntheses found in these three essays will stimulate other questions and objections, and it is in this that I see the principal merit of their posthumous publication. These lectures show the breadth of Herlihy's historical *oeuvre*, from broad sweeps in reinterpreting Western Civilization to the creative use of quantitative methods to ferret out new facts from previously untapped medieval sources.[62] At the same time, these essays underscore what Anthony Molho has recently claimed about David Herlihy and the direction of late medieval history:

> The economic and social consequences of the ecological balance have been studied systematically only in the past quarter century. However recent, these studies have themselves transformed our vision of European society at the close of the Middle Ages. No scholar has contributed more effectively to this view than David Herlihy.[63]

 ONE

Bubonic Plague:
Historical Epidemiology and
the Medical Problems

The Black Death of 1348 and 1349, and the recurrent epidemics
of the fourteenth and fifteenth centuries, were the most devastating natural disasters ever to strike Europe.[1] We cannot cite
exact losses; there are no global figures. The populations of some
cities and villages, in areas as far removed from each other as
England and Italy, fell in the late decades of the fourteenth century by 70 or 80 percent.[2] The more we learn of the late medieval
collapse in human numbers, the more awesome it appears.
Europe about 1420 could have counted barely more than a third
of the people it contained one hundred years before.

This was Europe's greatest known ecological disaster, and also
the last of such magnitude it has had to endure. The epidemics
of modern history seem mild when compared with the fury of
the Black Death. A principal thesis here is that the two salient
characteristics of the population collapse of the late Middle
Ages—Europe's deepest and also its last—are not unrelated.
The devastating plagues elicited a social response that protected
the European community from comparable disasters until the
present.

The great medieval epidemics have in recent years attracted
considerable attention from historians. There are several reasons

for this. In part it reflects the contemporary effort of historians to recapture more of the past than their predecessors accomplished. Ultimately, they would like to reconstruct the entire environment, the total life situation, that prevailed in past epochs. In this quest for total history, they of course include the cultural climate—ideas, ideologies, beliefs, myths and values—that circumscribed human life. But the physical environment also demands consideration. How did human communities interact with their natural surroundings? What were the ecological systems of the past? Indisputably, microorganisms play a crucial role in all systems of human ecology. Parasitic microbes also have a history, dark to be sure, but intimately connected with that of their human hosts.

Then too, current interest in past plagues owes a good deal to present concerns about public health. One hundred years ago, the great bacteriologist Louis Pasteur declared: "It is now in the power of man to cause all parasitic diseases to disappear from the world."[3] The science he helped found went on to spectacular successes. But the victory has not proved total, and the microbiotic legions have proved to be unexpectedly resilient. The disease called AIDS, mysteriously appearing, was once mostly limited to certain clearly delineated social groups; but it now seems poised to make forays into the general population. Almost all current descriptions of AIDS, if they are written with some historical awareness, carry allusions to earlier epidemics, and to the king of them all, the Black Death. An AIDS researcher at New York University was quoted as claiming that this new disease will "probably prove to be the plague of the millennium."[4] Not long ago, the accounts of the medieval epidemics, preserved in the great warehouse of history, were regarded as irrelevant to modern life. AIDS has made them relevant again. How do people behave, when their environment becomes life-threatening? History here can serve; it remembers how societies coped in the past with the threat of *mors repentina,* unexpected death.

The results of much recent research on the medieval epidemics and their impact can be summarized. Some personal interpretations about what they were and what they did can be offered. The plague itself cannot be directly examined. Always it is filtered through the reports of witnesses, who might have been unperceptive, uninformed, gullible, panicked, or eager to prove that they had read earlier accounts of dramatic mortalities. For example, medical writers of late antiquity and the early Middle Ages recognized only one type of epidemic disease marked by only one kind of symptom, inflammations, boils, or buboes in the area of the groin.[5] The authority of the ancients may have blinded later witnesses to other symptoms, indicating the presence of other types of epidemic disease. Then too, the plagues touched every aspect of social life, but in doing so they became intertwined with every other social influence. From the matrix of forces shaping the late medieval world, it is impossible to factor out those attributable to plague alone. The significance of plague in medieval history can be easily exaggerated. But more easily still, it can be, and usually has been, ignored. It did not of itself redirect European history. But neither can the new directions of European history be appreciated without recognition of its role.

What was the Black Death really?

The name, Black Death, was never used in the Middle Ages.[6] Apparently the first to coin the term were Danish and Swedish chroniclers of the sixteenth century. "Black" here connoted not a symptom or a color but "terrible," "dreadful." The name was slow to achieve currency in the other north-European languages, German and English.

Then, in the early nineteenth century, much as today, a new disease awakened interest in the old. Cholera invaded Europe and America; though not extraordinarily contagious, it was ghastly in the sufferings it imposed. In 1832 a German physician named J. F. K. Hecker, directly motivated by the menace of cholera, published an essay on the pestilence of 1348 and 1349. Dr. Hecker expressly intended his essay for "medical doctors and educated non-doctors." The title he chose for his essay was *Der schwarze Tod,* the Black Death.[7] The essay won immediate attention, thanks largely to the panic which cholera was everywhere inciting. It was quickly translated into English in 1833, and was several times reprinted in the nineteenth century.[8] Hecker's large readership, especially among doctors, helped make "Black Death" the standard term in English for the great pestilence of 1348. But he may not have been the sole source of its diffusion. In 1823 the wife of an Anglican minister, Elizabeth Cartwright Penrose, wrote a history of England, ostensibly for the instruction of her own children.[9] The work, which purported to record conversations between a mother and her children about English history, achieved the status of a school textbook and was many times reprinted, both in England and America. She too uses the term Black Death to describe the pestilence of 1349, but gives no source for her choice. At all events, her textbook made the name familiar to the schooled population of England and America, even as Dr. Hecker established its usage in savant circles. However, the name has remained primarily a north-European coinage; even today, for example, it is rarely encountered in Italian works, and its occasional appearance primarily reflects Anglo-American influences.

The modern medical diagnosis of the disease is chiefly based on research and clinical observations made at the turn of the last century. Most notably in 1894, in China, the plague emerged from the inland provinces of Hunan and Canton, where it was endemic, to attack the port city of Hong Kong. Classically a water-borne disease, it went on to menace port cities and their hinterlands all over the world. A Swiss microbiologist named Alexandre Yersin, who had trained at the Pasteur Institute at Paris, was then serving in the French colonial service in Indo-China. He hurried to Hong Kong and set up a laboratory there, in hopes of containing the disease before it struck southeast Asia. In 1894 he isolated the bacillus and went on to develop a serum for the treatment of plague.[10] The disease is consequently called *pasteurella pestis,* after the Pasteur Institute, or, more commonly today, *Yersinia pestis,* after Alexandre Yersin.

The efforts to contain the disease at Hong Kong were not entirely successful. In 1896 the plague, apparently brought from the Chinese port, struck the city of Bombay and an adjoining district called the presidency. From India and China we possess extensive clinical descriptions of the character and course of the epidemic. Raging at Bombay until 1899, it flickered sporadically in other ports—Oporto in Portugal, Glasgow in Scotland, and Sidney in Australia. Even American ports, such as San Francisco, passed uneasy moments. But except in India, it could not break through the defenses which centuries of struggle had raised against it.

In current understanding, plague is primarily a disease of small mammals.[11] It survives indefinitely in populations of wild rodents—prairie dogs, ground squirrels, marmots, and the like. These wild populations are its natural reservoirs. But it can infect rodents, such as grey rats, that live in or close to human habitations. Humans, on the other hand, are always its secondary, almost accidental victims. Its principal vector, the rat flea, prefers to avoid human beings. The flea will leave the infected rat only when the rodent dies and grows cold, and will seek out a human host only when a live, warm rat is not accessible.

Modern clinical observations of the disease identify three types of plague, though not all are due to the same bacillus. These are bubonic, septicemic, and pneumonic. The presence of bacilli, whether in glandular inflammations called buboes, in the blood, or in the sputum, is the basis for this differentiation. The most common of the three types is bubonic. To judge from the Chinese and Indian data, bubonic plague accounts for three-quarters and more of all cases.

Injected into its human host by the flea's bite, the plague bacilli pass an incubation period of from two to eight days. A soaring fever then ensues, climbing as high as 105 degrees, and it is often accompanied by convulsions, vomiting, giddiness, intolerance to light, and agonizing pain in the limbs. The patient frequently appears dazed or stupefied. On the second or third day after the inception of fever, swellings, about the size of an egg or small apple, occur in the lymph glands closest to the location of the initial bite, usually in the groin, but sometimes in the armpits or the neck. These are the famous buboes, and much pain accompanies their formation. Left alone, they will usually suppurate and burst. Petechiae, small crimson or livid spots, appear on the patient's skin in severe cases. If the patient does not succumb to exhaustion, heart failure, or internal hemorrhage, convalescence begins after eight to ten days.

The more lethal forms of plague, apparently always fatal, are the septicemic and pneumonic. At the onset of septicemic plague the bacilli invade the bloodstream in such massive numbers that the patient dies before the buboes can form—typically within 24 to 36 hours. Pneumonic plague is, as its name implies, a form of pneumonia triggered by the plague bacillus. The patient breathes rapidly and must gasp for air, produces a watery and profuse expectoration, and develops edema of the lungs. Alone among the types of plague, pneumonic can pass directly from one human to another. Drops of saliva carry the bacillus, and are spread about by coughing, sneezing, or simple conversation.

How well do the etiology and epidemiology of modern plague fit what we know about the medieval epidemics? In the now largely accepted reconstruction, the original reservoir of the medieval disease was the population of wild rodents, specifically marmots or a kind of large marmot called tarbagan, that inhabited the arid plateau of central Asia, the area that was the Soviet Republic of Turkestan. There the disease was, and is, enzootic. But for centuries it left untouched the indigenous, nomadic populations. Apparently rat fleas do not like the smell of horses, and the nomads did not remain in close proximity to infected rodent populations. Several events disturbed the ecological stability of the area in the early fourteenth century. Western chroniclers speak of earthquakes and volcanic eruptions in eastern lands, but their true effects are impossible to determine.[12] Social and political changes were probably more important, or at least more visible. A great silk route connecting Europe with China ran through the region, and traffic across it had grown intense by the early fourteenth century. The commercial towns of Italy were eager to trade with fabled Cathay. From the middle of the thirteenth century, Italians founded colonies on the northern littoral of the Black Sea. From these stations missionaries and merchants, Marco Polo among them, successfully traversed the overland highway, all the way to China. To serve its flourishing commerce, post stations were set up along its course. Towns grew there too, bringing with them complex social and political organizations. The settled inhabitants of towns were apparently more vulnerable to plague infection than the wandering nomads.

Some years ago, a Soviet archeologist named Khvolson excavated a cemetery of Nestorian Christians at a town called Issyk Kul, south of Lake Balkhash. He noted heavy mortalities in 1338–39; three gravestones actually identify plague as the cause of death. This seems to be the first appearance of the epidemic that would devastate Europe.

In the early 1340s the plague, moving westward along the silk route, penetrated the Mongol Khanate of the Golden Horde, with its capital at Sarai on the lower Volga River. But it still was contained within the great Eurasian landmass. To spread widely and quickly, and to take on the proportions of a true pandemic, the plague must cross water. Contact with water ignites its latent powers, like oil thrown upon fire.

It struck water at the Black Sea port of Kaffa, modern Theodosia, in the Crimea. The Genoese had founded the colony about 1266. A khan of the Golden Horde, named Yanibeg, besieged the town in 1343 and again in 1345–46. In a determined effort to take the town, he catapulted the bodies of plague victims over its walls. The Genoese hurriedly dumped these biological bombs into the sea. But the infection caught on.[13] In entering Kaffa, the disease broke onto the far-flung trading network of the Genoese. The coastline of the entire Mediterranean Sea now lay open to attack.

The now rapid diffusion of the plague through Europe followed a characteristic pattern. In a first phase, the plague leapt from infected port to one still uncontaminated. It then fell quiescent for a while, usually during the cold months of winter. Then, in a second phase, usually in the following spring, it invaded the hinterland and simultaneously moved by sea to the next accessible port. These again served as bases, for forays inland, and for farther leaps by sea. The deadly cycle was renewed.

Thus, in 1347, plague leapt from Kaffa to Constantinople and then to Cairo and Messina in Sicily. A Byzantine observer noted its pattern of infesting first the ports, then the hinterland: "A plague attacked almost all the sea coasts of the world and killed most of the people. For it swept not only through Pontus, Thrace and Macedonia, but even Greece, Italy and all the Islands, Egypt, Lybia, Judea and Syria."[14] From Messina, it was carried in early 1348 to Pisa, Genoa, Venice, Marseilles, and Barcelona, paused, and then moved like a well-drilled army forth from its maritime bases into the hinterland. It struck Florence in April of 1348; Giovanni Boccaccio, in the preface to the *Decameron*, has left a classical description of its devastation.

In the north of Europe, the plague reached Melcombe Regis,

the present Weymouth, in the shire of Dorset in southwest England, in June of 1348. Apparently, it rode the merchant ships coming from the Gascon ports of Bordeaux or Bayonne, then under English rule.[15] Again it paused, smoldering over the winter. But in 1349 it flared with power, raged through Britain as far north as the Scottish highlands, and wrecked havoc on the eastern half of Ireland. Bubonic plague is today regarded as a tropical disease, but it had no difficulty crossing the waters of the North and Baltic seas, that is, the northern Mediterranean. Movement from port to port, respite, then invasion of the hinterland: the familiar pattern holds. Calais, Bergen, Cologne, Copenhagen, Lübeck, and Novgorod in distant Russia now caught the infection from incoming ships. And it advanced deep into the eastern part of the Continent. In 1352 it struck Moscow; both the grand duke of Muscovy and the patriarch of the Russian Church were counted among its victims. It swept still farther south, apparently as far as Kiev. Launched at Kaffa in the Crimea, and now attaining Kiev some 700 kilometers to the north, the plague almost closed a deadly noose around Europe.

Was this *Yersinia pestis,* bubonic plague as it is known through recent occurrences? Most historians think so. Many witnesses mention boils or buboes found upon the bodies of its victims. For example, a Florentine chronicler, Matteo Villani, gives the following description of the Black Death:

> It was a plague that touched people of every condition, age and sex. They began to spit blood and then they died—some immediately, some in two or three days, and some in a longer time. And it happened that whoever cared for the sick caught the disease from them or, infected by the corrupt air, became rapidly ill and died in the same way. Most had swellings in the groin, and many had them in the left and right armpits and in other places; one could almost always find an unusual swelling somewhere on the victim's body.[16]

As buboes are the classic symptom and even give their name to plague, this now conventional diagnosis appears well founded.

But many puzzles remain. Perhaps the biggest puzzle touches on a characteristic of bubonic epidemiology which the sources do not mention. To my knowledge, not a single Western chronicler notes the occurrence of an epizootic, the massive mortalities of rats, which ought to have preceded and accompanied the human plague. Humans, in the classic bubonic epidemiology, can contract the disease only from a dying rodent; unless the rodents die, the human population remains untouched.[17]

Epizootics were very visible during the observed plagues of China and of India. As one witness at Canton in 1894 reported, "the rats . . . would come out of their holes in broad daylight even, and tumble about in a dazed condition and die."[18] One Chinese official collected 22,000 dead rats—we aren't told why.[19] Albert Camus, in *La Peste*, his fictional account of the plague in a North African city, appropriately makes the observed sickness and death of rats the first indication of the approaching human epidemic.[20] But witnesses watching the disease in its repeated onslaughts over centuries of European history miss this omen. Or did they miss it; did it in fact occur?

The problematic connection of epidemic to a preceding epizootic highlights another puzzle: how could the disease have spread so quickly and so powerfully, over land as well as water? Humans cannot infect other humans,[21] and the grey rat is allegedly a homebody that will not migrate spontaneously. The mechanisms by which bubonic plague diffuses in a human population are singularly cumbersome. Some historians avoid these difficulties by attributing the high mortalities to the pneumonic form of the disease, which could be carried and spread by humans.[22] But this does not remove all the difficulties. The great medieval epidemics usually show a pronounced seasonal rhythm. Typically, they gathered strength as the weather warmed, and reached maximum virulence in late summer or early autumn, when tempera-tures were at their warmest. Cool weather in late autumn and winter dissipated their power. This cycle does not suggest a form of pneumonia. Pneumonic plague should have worsened in win-ter, when people stayed indoors, huddled around the sources of heat and breathing the same stale air.

Nor does a diagnosis of bubonic plague fit all the symptoms noted in the contemporary accounts. Guy de Chauliac, a physi-cian and surgeon serving the papal court at Avignon, identifies two forms of the disease.[23] The first and more virulent of the two appeared early in 1348; it was marked by high fever and coughing of blood. Death came very quickly—in three days—and it was so contagious that the sick persons allegedly even passed on the infection by their glances alone. No buboes formed, and the symptoms more closely resemble those of galloping consumption than plague. The second type appeared later in the year and did produce buboes, but was less deadly and less contagious.[24] Another physician at Avignon, Raymond Chalin de Vinario (or Raymond Chalmel de Viviers who flourished between 1373 and 1388) mentions as symptomatic of the plague skin eruptions, *pustulae* or pustules which appeared in the groin, legs, head, arms, or shoulders.[25] They were livid in color, and numerous enough to form a rash over large areas of the body. The common people, he tells us, called this rash the "plague girdle."

In investigating the medical aspects of the plague, the great need is for clear and precise descriptions of the disease and its symptoms. The Black Death itself certainly inspired much closer inspection at the time of all the sick and dying and great interest in the nature of their illnesses. At Florence, for example, from at least 1377, the commune required that undertakers report all burials, which were entered into registers called *Libri dei morti*, "Books of the Dead."[26] From at least 1424, the Florentine un-dertakers were also reporting the apparent cause of death. Unhappily, they did so only occasionally, whenever plague was in the vicinity and an epidemic was feared. To identify those who died of plague, the scribes entered the words "di segno," "with the sign," in the margin alongside the burial entry, and for good measure added a big "P" in front of the names. They do not, however, state what they took to be the certain sign of death from plague.

What was this sign? Another kind of record carries many exact descriptions of medieval illnesses, but this has not, to my knowledge, been used in the study of historic diseases. These are the acts or processes used to judge candidates for sainthood.[27] Since the early thirteenth century, the papacy claimed the exclusive right to canonize saints. It created tribunals and set up elaborate procedures to judge the holiness of each reputed servant of God. An essential part of the process was proof that the candidate had worked miracles, either before or after death. Most miracles involved cures. Witnesses claiming that they had been healed or had seen a healing came forward, and their depositions draw a striking picture of medieval morbidity. Many such depositions are published, though usually only in part, in the great collection of hagiographic texts known as the *Acta Sanctorum*.[28]

Some saints were specialists in curing plague. One of them was Rose of Viterbo in Italy, who died about 1252. She lapsed into obscurity soon after her death, and no contemporary recorded her life. But the devastating epidemics inspired a frantic search for heavenly patrons. Rose was rediscovered when the great epidemic struck Viterbo in 1450, and she responded by effecting many cures. In gratitude for her help, the government pressured the Pope to initiate canonization procedures, and many citizens came forward to testify concerning recent cures.

Some depositions mention buboes. "In the year of the Lord 1448, in the month of July, a certain Angelina, daughter of Tozio Lorenzetti, of Viterbo, was gravely sick of pestilence, with two [buboes] in the groin and one in the arm."[29] Others refer to the disease "which in the vulgar tongue is called *aguinaglia.*"[30] This old Italian word for the plague derives from the term for groin. But many others mention *fistulae,* skin lesions of some sort found typically on the shins.[31] As the *fistulae* remained for years—one deposition mentions eight—the illness may have been a form of tuberculosis rather than plague.

Unlike the Florentine undertakers, the witnesses of Viterbo describe the "sign" that infallibly identified death from plague. It was not the buboes. "Thus all the signs that death was coming upon her were seen, especially since throughout her whole body the signs which are vulgarly called *lenticulae* appeared to such an extent that everyone despaired of her life."[32] Another deposition relates: "and already the signs of death had appeared upon her, which are vulgarly called *lenticulae.*" We read further: "Peter Dominus, when he was about six years old in 1450, was racked by an intolerable fever, and the sign came upon him."[33] But his nurse and relatives forced the sick boy to drink water that had washed Rose's hands (her body had been exhumed). "Without any delay the fever ceased together with the sign." The sign is not specified, but there is no mention of buboes.

The key word here, *lenticulae,* is the same as the vernacular Italian word, *lentiggini,* "freckles." The sense seems to be a rash or splotches formed of pustules or boils. Another deposition refers to *pestilentialis punturae,* "pestilential points."[34]

The "sign," in other words, which contemporaries took to be the surest indication of death from plague, was not the bubo,[35] but darkish points or pustules which covered large areas of the body. Cases of true bubonic plague sometimes produce petechiae, but the symptom does not seem universal or even common, and could not be taken as the sure sign of plague infection.[36]

Can the epidemics of the Middle Ages then be medically identified? In a book published in 1984, an epidemiologist named

Graham Twigg tentatively identified the medieval epidemics as anthrax.[37] Anthrax can produce the characteristic swellings which might be mistaken for buboes, and it can also come in pulmonary or pneumonic form. But historically, it has certainly never struck human populations in epidemic proportions.

We still have much to learn of the etiology and epidemiology of medieval *pestis*. It is at least certain it comes in epidemic outbursts. It rages in warm weather, and this suggests some association with contaminated food and water. Its victims always develop a high fever and sometimes delirium. Buboes frequently appear, but the most common sign of a plague mortality are *lenticulae*, spots or pustules covering large areas of the body. Unfortunately for certain identification, many fevers share these traits, but no one of them, including bubonic plague, shows them all. A fulminant rash appears in cases of typhoid and typhus fever, and both can sustain epidemics. Other symptoms—the presence of skin lesions over long periods, the spitting of blood, even inflammation of the lymph glands—suggest forms of tuberculosis. Perhaps different diseases were responsible for the epidemics of different years. Perhaps too they sometimes worked together synergistically to produce the staggering mortalities. Finally, the plague bacilli may have taken on variant forms, aping other diseases in the pathology they produced. Microbiologists have identified at least two such variants.[38] One they call *Yersinia pseudo-tuberculosis*, because of the similarity of its pathology to true tuberculosis. A second is *Yersinia enterocolita*, which, like typhoid or typhus, is primarily seated in the lower digestive track. But it remains hard to know whether these mutants existed in the Middle Ages.

The question as to the true nature of the great medieval epidemics remains open. But three conclusions seem justified. The present understanding of the medical nature of the plague is inadequate. But we have not exhausted the sources that record its symptoms, and here the depositions taken in processes of canonization appear especially promising. And the plague bacillus itself seems not to have been stable, and probably has not even today exhausted its capacity to evolve into new forms. It is not at all certain that the diseases we observe today are the same that troubled our ancestors.

Why were the medieval populations so vulnerable to these killing diseases? Many historians, dissatisfied with medical explanations, have looked to social factors to explain the catastrophic losses. Two proposed explanations have elicited much lively discussion. One is based on Malthusian principles, the other on Marxist.

In 1798 the English clergyman Thomas Malthus published the first edition of his influential *Essay on the Principle of Population*.[39] In it he concluded that human populations would tend to expand up to and beyond the limits of their food supplies. When they passed those limits, a reckoning was inevitable. The reckoning took the form of famines, epidemics, wars, and the soaring mortality resulting from them. These "positive checks," as he called them, violently reduced the community's numbers to a size that its resources could support.

Several historians maintain that the great population debacle of the fourteenth century was itself a classical Malthusian crisis, triggered by excessive numbers of people. Among the most prominent advocates of such a view have been the late M. M. Postan in England, and Emmanuel Le Roy Ladurie in France.[40] Their conclusion—that Europe was overpopulated on the eve of the Black Death—rests on two types of evidence, direct and indirect. The direct evidence is the sheer size that many European communities had attained by ca. 1300. To cite only one out of many possible examples, the Italian region of Tuscany at its medieval height, according to the estimates of Enrico Fiumi, was inhabited by probably two million people.[41] It would not hold such numbers again until after 1850. With its poorly productive economy and stagnant technology, how could medieval Tuscany have supported so big a population? It could not support it, the argument runs, and famines and wars, and the Black Death itself, were the consequences.

The indirect evidence of overpopulation rests primarily on the history of cereal prices and the occurrences of famine. Basic foodstuffs were costly in the late thirteenth and early fourteenth centuries. One price list from Norfolk, from 1290 and 1348, shows there were nineteen years when wheat prices were so high as to indicate dearth and hunger.[42] In Languedoc between 1302 and 1348, the years of scarcity were twenty, nearly the same as the twenty-seven years of adequate food supplies.[43] More dramatic than price series in measuring population pressures against the food supply were the appearances of true famines. In northern Europe, a major famine, known traditionally as the "great hunger," persisted for three years, from 1314 to 1317. Famine struck also right before the Black Death, in 1346 and 1347, in both north and south. A Florentine, Giovanni Morelli, attributes the high mortality of the Black Death to famine the previous year. Not twenty out of one hundred people, he reports, had bread. The rest lived on herbs and vile plants; grazing like cattle, they filled the countryside. "Think," he explains, "how their bodies were affected."[44] In France, Simon de Couvin affirmed: "The one who was poorly nourished by unsubstantial food fell victim to the merest breath of the disease; the impoverished crowd of common folk died a welcome death, since for them life was death."[45]

Malthusian pressures against the food supply are very apparent in pre-plague Europe, as a huge population struggled to live on scant resources. But was there a Malthusian reckoning? There are grounds for disbelief. European population movements in the thirteenth and fourteenth centuries do not adhere very closely to

Malthusian predictions. It is not known when the medieval population peaked; the documents are full of gaps, and regional variations undoubtedly were considerable. It is, however, certain that European population levels were already high, at least from the last decades of the thirteenth century. Hence the Black Death did not strike against a population recklessly adding to its size, but one that had been stable for fifty to a hundred years before 1348. If the Black Death was a response to excessive human numbers, it should have arrived several decades earlier. Moreover, if Europe was overpopulated in 1348, was it still overpopulated later in the century, when the number of people had fallen to half of what it had been? And yet the population continued to fall. It did not stabilize until the opening decades of the fifteenth century, and even then remained stagnant at very low levels for another fifty years. Not until 1460 or 1470 does it again begin to grow. These movements of deep decline, long stability, and slow recovery are inexplicable, on the assumption that resources and their availability alone dominate demographic cycles. A British historian, Bruce M. S. Campbell, who studied the Black Death in an English village, Coltishall, concludes: "The extraordinarily prolonged demographic recession which followed the advent of plague at Coltishall, as elsewhere in the country, defies simple Malthusian . . . logic."[46]

The role of famines in affecting population movements is also problematic. The many famines preceding the Black Death, even the "great hunger" of 1314 to 1317, did not result in any appreciable reduction in population levels. They pale besides plague as a waster of human numbers. Even in modern European history, with the exception of the potato blight in Ireland in 1847, famines seem never to have taken exceptional tolls, and never to have reversed the dominant demographic trend.[47] Nor do there seem to be direct linkages between famine and plague, malnutrition and disease. Under certain conditions, malnutrition can even

33

work as a prophylactic against infection. Bacteria need many of the same nutrients as their human hosts. When those nutrients are lacking, the germs cannot multiply. It has even been claimed, although not convincingly proved, that persons prone to anemia—chiefly menstruating women and growing children—enjoyed a certain immunity against plague.[48] The bacilli found insufficient free iron in the blood to support their own fast multiplication. Campbell is doubtless correct in his further conclusion: "none [of the fourteenth-century plagues] had anything whatever to do with prevailing economic conditions. Plague is an exogenous variable and as such is neither easily nor happily accommodated within an exclusively Malthusian or Marxist interpretation of events."[49]

There are also conceptual difficulties with the Malthusian argument. When is a community overpopulated? Presumably, when it fails to maintain some known standard of subsistence. But that is necessarily a relative, not an absolute measure, which will vary from community to community and from period to period. A count of the hearths of Tuscany at about 1300 makes the region appear very crowded indeed to a modern observer. But what did this mean in real terms? Many Tuscans went hungry, and many were undoubtedly malnourished. But somehow people managed to survive. Until the arrival of plague, the region held its numbers rather well.

Malthus, in sum, seems mistaken in his conclusion that populations grow relentlessly,[50] and that violent adjustments downward have to occur. The medieval experience shows us not a Malthusian crisis but a stalemate, in the sense that the community was maintaining at stable levels very large numbers over a lengthy period. In Tuscany, under these crowded conditions, many lived in misery, but somehow they coped. Malthusian deadlock, rather than crisis, seems the more appropriate term to describe the demographic state of Europe before the epidemics.

A final weakness of the Malthusian interpretation is its failure to consider divisions within medieval society, especially between rich and poor. Surely rich and poor were not subject to the dearth of resources in the same way. Marxist critics in particular have dwelt upon this omission, even as they propose their own explanation for the crisis of the closing Middle Ages.

Marxism makes the balance of classes and the class struggle the chief motor of historical change. Marxist historiography has been from its origins antagonistic to Malthusianism in any form. Exploitation, not overcrowding, explains human misery, and insurrection, not contraception, is the right response. Among the chief architects and advocates of a Marxist interpretation have been an American, Robert Brenner, and a Frenchman, Guy Bois. In a article published in 1976 in the journal *Past and Present,* rich in theory though not in data, Brenner launched a spirited criticism of the Malthusian thesis.[51] Basically he argued that the plague was common to all Europe, but social and economic changes were very different from one region to another. Malthus was not the master of the game; Marx was. Only social structure can explain the regional evolutions. Plagues came and went, but classes and their tensions remained. Late medieval society carried this mark, not the sign of the plague, upon its body.

Guy Bois, in a study of eastern Normandy in the late Middle Ages, published in 1976 and now translated into English, has developed the most elaborate Marxian model of social and political change across the late Middle Ages.[52] His data show the same shocking reduction in population with which we are familiar. Between the early fourteenth and the early fifteenth century, the population of eastern Normandy collapsed by 70 or 80 percent. Were plagues responsible? Bois thinks not. They occurred in the middle of the fourteenth century, and the population was still declining afterwards. They also occurred in the early sixteenth century, and the population continued to grow. They did not, in other words, redirect the dominant trends. The real driver in this demographic debacle was a crisis in the social order, what Bois calls the crisis of feudalism.

To understand that crisis it is necessary first to appreciate the "feudal mode of production," its characteristics and its contradictions. The basic unit of production in this feudal mode was the small peasant farm, worked with an essentially stagnant technology. The only growth the system allowed was extensive, that is, the expansion of the cultivated area and the multiplication of farm units. But growth under the feudal mode was subject to the law of diminishing returns. As cultivation extended onto poorer soils, so the returns to the average family farm necessarily diminished. In eastern Normandy, the lords monopolized political power and used it to extract rents from the peasants. But the peasants still controlled actual production and the distribution of the harvests. This was a fundamental flaw, or contradiction, in Marxist terminology, in the system. As peasant income diminished, they paid lower and lower rents; the support of their own families had first claim upon them. Initially, the lords did not suffer from declining per-family rents. The continuing expansion of the cultivated area and the multiplication of rent-paying units at first compensated for the lower rents that each family delivered.

But at a certain moment, which Bois dates to about 1315, the decline in per-family rents overcame the increase coming from the larger number of farms. From that moment on, the lords faced continuous shrinkage in the total revenues they collected. Bois calls this a "crisis of feudal rent," and claims it engendered a crisis of feudalism itself.

The lords had to seek alternate sources of revenue. They took to robbery and pillage—the direct expropriation of peasant wealth. They also hired themselves out as mercenaries. And they pressured their overlords, notably the king, to wage wars against their neighbors. In war they hoped to capture a wealthy opponent, hold him for high ransom, and thus repair their fortunes.

In sum, the crisis of feudalism provoked the interminable wars of the late Middle Ages, many of which were thinly disguised pillaging expeditions. But the waging of wars required that the king enlarge his powers and his fiscal resources. State taxes tended to replace feudal rents as the chief form of peasant expropriation. Military bands ravaged the countryside, and tax collectors took what the pillagers left behind. Little wonder, then, that the population collapsed, but this was the effect and not the cause of the crisis in feudalism.

Sensitive to class divisions, Bois's model offers a complex, subtle, and illuminating analysis of late medieval social trends in eastern Normandy. But it does not seem to be as free of Malthusian influences as the author contends. The balance between population and land determines per-farm productivity and the level of rents. Pressures against the land—must we not call them Malthusian?—lower farm productivity and directly engender the crisis in feudal rent. That crisis might be considered a Malthusian reckoning in another form. Bois even concedes that demographic movements seem to follow "a law of their own," and this seems tantamount to admitting that not even Marxist analysis can control the total picture.

Then, too, the crisis of feudalism might well be regarded as an appropriate model of social change in late medieval eastern Normandy. But what about other regions in Europe, such as Tuscany, which possessed very different economic and social systems? Tuscany, for example, included one of Europe's largest cities, Florence, which lived from international commerce, banking, and manufacture. Even its agriculture was very different from that found in Normandy. Did a crisis of feudalism occur there too? The merchant elites of Italy did not respond to falling agrarian rents by resorting to pillage and to mercenary service; they were in fact reluctant fighters.[53] And yet the population movements in the two regions are very similar. What did the Florentine metropolis and the Norman villages truly share, except the experience of plague?

This then is how several historians have viewed the state of Europe before the plague. To my mind, the best reading of the evidence is the following. European population had grown to extraordinary levels during the central Middle Ages, but the result was not a Malthusian reckoning or crisis, but a deadlock. In spite of frequent famine and widespread hunger, the community in ca. 1300 was successfully holding its numbers. It is likely that this equilibrium could have been maintained for the indefinite future. It is likely too that the Malthusian stalemate might have paralyzed social movement and improvement. Then the plague struck. It appeared as an exogenous intervention; it owed its power not to social factors but to its still obscure nature. And it devastated Europe. But in spite of the havoc it wrought, it did a service to the West. It broke the Malthusian deadlock that medieval growth had created and which might have impeded further growth in different forms. It guaranteed that in the generations after 1348 Europe would not simply continue the pattern of society and culture of the thirteenth century. It assured that the Middle Ages would be the middle, not the final, phase in Western development.

 TWO

The New Economic and Demographic System

Europe, before the Black Death assaulted it, was a very crowded continent. But despite the pressure on the land, stability prevailed. For fifty, perhaps one hundred years before 1348, the population had registered no significant gains. Food costs were high and famines frequent, but they did not send the population plummeting. The economy was saturated; nearly all available resources were committed to the effort of producing the food, clothing, and shelter needed to support the packed communities. Agriculture was mobilized for the production of cereals, the basic foodstuff, and cultivation had extended to the limits of the workable land. Undoubtedly, vast numbers of Europeans lived in deep deprivation. But despite misery and hunger, the pressure of human numbers went unrelieved. The civilization that this economy supported, the civilization of the central Middle Ages, might have maintained itself for the indefinite future. That did not happen; an exogenous factor, the Black Death, broke the Malthusian deadlock. And in doing so it gave to Europeans the chance to rebuild their society along much different lines.

The salient effects of the Black Death on the economic and demographic systems of medieval Europe can be described with some certainty: the surviving evidence is reasonably abundant.

Many contemporary witnesses commented on human behavior at the workplace and marketplace in the wake of epidemics. Even some quantitative data, chiefly price citations, have survived. Several historians have used these materials, and they are in considerable agreement as to the nature and direction of economic change in the late Middle Ages. The demographic system operating in medieval Europe is much harder to investigate. Records that could tell us how medieval people married and reproduced are notoriously scarce and nearly always subject to diverse interpretations. Nonetheless, I shall argue here that the demographic system of the Middle Ages, which I envisage as formed of the relationships among deaths, marriages, and births, all subject to the economic performance, was also profoundly altered in this period of plague.

In considering the effect of the epidemics upon the economy, it is necessary to distinguish short-term and long-term repercussions. The chief short-term repercussion was shock. And shock in turn broke the continuities of economic life and disrupted established routines of work and service. The high mortalities left numerous posts in society unfilled and services unperformed. According to Boccaccio, many concurred "that against plagues no medicine was better than or even equal to simple flight."[1] The retreat of the ten young Florentines to a country villa, portrayed in the *Decameron,* is a fictional but still typical example of this popular response to epidemic. The desertion of towns and cities, through death and flight, threatened communities with chaos.

How, under such conditions, could an organized economy be maintained? Many contemporaries affirm that it was not maintained, that workers either died or fled their posts, or simply refused to perform, preferring to indulge their appetites while they still had the chance. Peasants, according to Boccaccio, "just like the townspeople became lax in their ways and neglected their chores as if they expected death that very day."[2] A French poet,

Guillaume de Machaut, describes the breakdown of the rural economy:

> For many have certainly
> Heard it commonly said
> How in one thousand three hundred and forty nine
> Out of one hundred there remained but nine.
> Thus it happened that for lack of people
> Many a splendid farm was left untilled,
> No one plowed the fields
> Bound the cereals and took in the grapes,
> Some gave triple salary
> But not for one denier was twenty [enough]
> Since so many were dead . . .[3]

He goes on to say that the animals roamed untended in the fields, as the lords could hire no shepherds.

The epidemics also greatly enlarged the demand for certain types of services. The records mention most often the need for gravediggers, physicians, and priests.

Gravediggers gained a special prominence at a time when people died each day by the hundreds. The task of burying the dead apparently gave employment to marginal social groups, poor rustics, beggars, and the urban jobless. Boccaccio implies that gravediggers who worked for pay were unknown at Florence before the Black Death. He calls them "a species of vulture born from the lowly."[4]

Physicians too were in demand. Boccaccio again laments that "the numbers [of physicians] had increased enormously because the ranks of the qualified were invaded by people, both men and women, who had never received any training in medicine."[5] His allusion to women carers of the sick is especially noteworthy. Another profession whose numbers proved inadequate for the services required was the clergy. Many priests had died, and many fled the contagion. Who would administer the Church's last rites

to the many who were dying? In January 1349, Ralph of Shrewsbury, the bishop of Wells and Bath in England, gave these instruc-
tions to his flock:

> The continuous pestilence of the present day, which is spreading
> far and wide, has left many parish churches and other livings in our
> diocese without parson or priest to care for their parishioners.
> Since no priests can be found who are willing, whether out of zeal
> and devotion or in exchange for a stipend, to take on the pastoral
> care of these aforesaid places, to visit the sick and administer to
> them the sacraments of the Church (perhaps for fear of infection
> and contagion), we understand that many people are dying
> without the sacrament of Penance . . . all men, in particular those
> who are now sick or should fall sick in the future, . . . if they are on
> the point of death and cannot secure the services of a priest, then
> they should make confession to each other, as is permitted in the
> teaching of the Apostles, whether to a layman or, if no man is
> present, even to a woman.[6]

The Church was traditionally suspicious of laymen and, in
particular, of women assuming pastoral functions or adminis-
tering the sacraments. In this instance, as plague thinned the
cadre of priests, the bishop of Wells and Bath had no choice.

The legal systems of late medieval Europe also had to respond
to the extraordinary social situation created by an epidemic.
Under conditions of plague, certain "privileges," as they were
known in the legal language, went into effect.[7] Women, for
example, could now serve as witnesses, and scribes not formally
admitted into the guild of notaries could draw up legal contracts.
Society needed certain services, and at these moments of crisis it
had to allow even the unlicensed or people believed to be incom-
petent to perform them.

Over the long term, the relaxation of the pressure of human
numbers created serious problems for the economy. The chief
problems were the drastic decrease in the number of workers, and

the abbreviated span of years over which they remained productive. The plagues radically reduced the average duration of life. To the best of our knowledge, life expectancies in the good years of the thirteenth century were between 35 and 40 years.[8] The ferocious epidemics of the late fourteenth century cut that figure to below 20; after 1400, as the population achieved a new equilibrium at very low levels, it extended to about 30 years. These figures necessarily affected the balances between young and old, and also between producers and dependents.

At Florence, a survey redacted in 1427 to 1430, called the Catasto, gives the ages of a large population of some 260,000 persons, in both cities and countryside.[9] It thus allows us to see the demographic contours of a community that had within the lifetime of some of its members endured repeated epidemics, including the Black Death of 1348. The age pyramid of the Tuscan population is very distorted. Old persons age 60 or above are surprisingly numerous. They constitute nearly 15 percent of the community—a proportion one would expect to find in a modern Western population with a low birth rate. How did Tuscany accumulate such large numbers of the aged? The answer seems to be that those in the last stages of life were in part survivors of a time when the total community was much bigger than in 1427. It also suggests that the plague preyed on the young rather than the mature. If a person survived one major epidemic, the chances improved that he or she would survive the next.

The number of children and youths up to age 19 was also very large, forming about 44 percent of the population—again a figure surprising for its size. So large a proportion of the young is normally found in a rapidly growing community, but Tuscany in 1427 was still barely maintaining its numbers. The adult and productive members of society, those between 20 and 59, were thus a minority of about 41 percent. Economists make use of a figure called a dependency ratio, the number of dependents in the community, the aged and the young, divided by the producers. In Tuscany in 1427, it was 1.44. Adults in their productive years thus bore a huge burden of dependents. Moreover, the wealth and effort invested in the rearing of children remained in significant measure wasted. Death ruthlessly thinned the ranks of the young before they could repay to society the resources and energy devoted to them.

High mortalities also cut short the careers of craftsmen and other professionals. Our best estimates are that the average duration of time spent in a career fell from about 32 years in the late thirteenth century to 26 in the last quarter of the fourteenth—a contraction of almost 20 percent.[10] The professions tried to compensate for reduced years of service by recruiting more new members than they had in the past, but they had to fish in a shrinking pool. Guild matriculation records tell us something of these problems of replacement under conditions of high mortality. At Florence, the matriculation lists of the guild of Por Santa Maria have survived seemingly intact from the early thirteenth century. The guild included but was not limited to silk merchants. The immediate response to epidemic was to increase the number admitted, in an obvious effort to replace those who had died.[11] Thus sixteen neophytes were matriculated in 1346, and 18 in 1347. The number jumped to 35 in the plague year of 1348, and reached 69 in 1349 and 67 in 1350, after which it slowly declined. The post-plague peaks of 69 and 67 represent the largest numbers admitted into the guild since 1328, twenty years previously. Over a longer term, the circulation of masters into and out of service greatly accelerated. In the 20 years immediately preceding the Black Death, from 1328 to 1347, the guild matriculated 730 new members. In the 20 following years, from 1348 to 1367, it brought in almost as many, 672, although the population was down by about one-third. In the early fifteenth century, from

1408 to 1427, it admitted 784, more than in the pre-plague period, although the city's population had fallen by two-thirds.

The most remarkable aspect of these and other matriculation lists we could cite is their apparent stability, in spite of soaring mortalities. Society tried to keep its occupational cadres constant in size, even though the total community and the pool of possible members were shrinking. The policy reflects in part social resistance to any disturbance or change, and in part too the premature deaths of the older masters. But to enlist constant numbers out of a shrinking pool, the guild had to spread its net broadly and bring in new apprentices with no previous family connection with the trade. The matriculation lists identify those among the neophytes whose father, uncle, or other close relative had practiced the trade. In the 25 years from 1406 to 1430, when the urban population was largely stable, 487 out of 938, or better than one out of two, claimed this association. In the 20 years after 1348, when the population was falling, 222 out of 672 were close relatives of a previous master, or one out of three. The depleted population forced the guild to extend its outreach. Probably in all occupations, the immediate post-plague period was an age of new men.

Short years of service before death intervened, rapid turnover in members, wide recruitment of new persons, affected the quality of the product or service the professions provided. The new masters of the art were trained less rigorously, and would accumulate less experience, before passing away. We take an example of what we mean from careers in religion, the best illuminated of all medieval professions.

In the opening decade of the fifteenth century, a Dominican friar, Giovanni di Carlo, from the convent of Santa Maria Novella in Florence, lamented how the religious orders had fallen into decadence. The chief reason he gives for their plight was the flooding of their ranks with young men, without the piety or learning of their predecessors. "How painful it is [he remarks] whenever men have been trained for many years and with great effort, that they pass away in scarcely one hour. All that diligence, which men previously applied in preparing and supporting outstanding careers, is rendered vain and useless."[12] The deterioration of skilled traditions was inevitable under conditions of high mortality—we shall see the pattern again in medieval cultural life. Europe at the time of plague, then, was a society reeling under repeated, powerful shocks; burdened with huge numbers of dependents; struggling with difficulty to maintain its occupational cadres; struggling also to uphold the quality of its skilled traditions.

But, over the long run, the breaking of the Malthusian deadlock conferred advantages too. Above all it freed resources. The collapse of population liberated land for uses other than the cultivation of grains. It could be turned to pasturage or to forests. In the past mills and mill sites had served predominantly for the grinding of grain. They now could be enlisted for other uses: the fulling of cloth, the operation of bellows, the sawing of wood. Even as the population shrank, the possibility of developing a more diversified economy was enhanced.

Price movements provide our best evidence of the directions of long-term economic trends in the late Middle Ages. The immediate effect of the Black Death upon prices was to produce general inflation. The Florentine Matteo Villani, writing in 1363, presents an apt analysis of price movements since 1348:

> It was thought that, given the lack of people, there ought to be a wealth of all the things which the earth produces. On the contrary, through men's ingratitude an unprecedented scarcity affected everything, and this continued for a long time. In certain lands, as we shall narrate, there were severe and unprecedented famines. And again, it was thought that there ought to be wealth and abundance of clothing, and of all the other things that the human body needs . . . but the opposite happened . . . Most things

cost two times or more what they cost before the epidemic. And labor, and the manufactures of every art and profession increased in disorderly fashion to double the price . . .[13]

This general inflation persisted until the last decades of the fourteenth century, and indicates that under the shock of plague production in town and countryside had fallen even more rapidly than the population.

Of all commodity prices, the most important, indeed the usual reference base for all others, was that of wheat. Wheat prices were everywhere high in Europe before the Black Death, reflecting the huge numbers of consumers and the intensive cultivation of grain, even on marginal soils. Wheat prices also increased after the Black Death. In England, Normandy, the Ile-de-France, Alsace, Flanders, and Spain, they remained high until about 1375.[14] In Tuscany the period of inflation persisted even longer, to about 1395.[15]

After 1375 or 1395, the price of wheat enters a phase of decline that persists for a century. Commodity prices now differentiate in their movements, and wheat prices form the lower blade of an opening scissors. Other food grains remain relatively buoyant. The price of barley, for example, stayed comparatively strong. This reflects its use in the brewing of beer. Perhaps the melancholy induced by the massive mortalities whetted the taste for beer, but it surely indicates an improving standard of living, and the better and more balanced diet of the people. The price of animal products—meat, sausage, cheese and the like—also remained relatively high. Europeans, even as their numbers declined, were living better. Many moralists complain of the extravagant tastes for food and attire which the lower social orders now manifested. Matteo Villani remarks: "The common people, by reason of the abundance and superfluity that they found, would no longer work at their accustomed trades; they wanted the dearest and most delicate foods . . . while children and common women clad themselves in all the fair and costly garments of the illustrious who had died."[16] Conspicuous consumption by the humble threatened to erase the visible marks of social distinctions and to undermine the social order. The response of the alleged prodigality in food and clothing was sumptuary laws, which governments enacted all over Europe in the fourteenth and fifteenth centuries. They tried to regulate fashions, such as the size of sleeves or the length of trains in women's dresses; meals, such as the food to be served at weddings; or customs, such as the number of mourners who could attend a funeral. The repetition of these laws suggests their futility. High wages to the poor and improved living standards came to be irremediable facts of late medieval economic and social life.

The price of wool moved erratically, but was strong enough to stimulate a widespread conversion from plowland to meadow. Moreover, one or two shepherds could guard hundreds of sheep, and this extensive use of the land saved the costs of hiring expensive tillers. Manufactured products also held their value better than wheat. But in the late Middle Ages, silk challenged wool as the most active branch of the textile production, again indicating smaller, but richer markets.

Besides commodity prices, the costs of the classical "factors of production"—labor, land, and capital—also responded to the new conditions. Of these production costs, the one most dramatically affected was that of labor. The falling numbers of renters and workers increased the strength of their negotiating position in bargaining with landlords and entrepreneurs. Agricultural rents collapsed after the Black Death, and wages in the towns soared, to two and even three times the levels they had held in the crowded thirteenth century. In 1363, Matteo Villani acutely observed:

> Serving girls and unskilled women with no experience in service and stable boys want at least 12 florins per year, and the most arrogant among them 18 or 24 florins per year, and so also nurses

and minor artisans working with their hands want three times or nearly the usual pay, and laborers on the land all want oxen and all seed, and want to work the best lands, and to abandon all others.[17]

Governments tried to cap the swell in wages and to shore up the shrinking rents. They sought to hold prices and wages to previous levels and insisted that workers accept any employment offered them. But they succeeded only in sowing discontent and in provoking social uprisings in city and countryside. The value of land diminished. We do not know a great deal of the costs of capital. But references in chronicles such as Matteo Villani's to the accumulation of inheritances suggests that capital too became cheaper in the contracting community.

The different movements of factor costs favored a policy of factor substitution. In particular, cheap land and capital were widely substituted for expensive labor. In effect, the conversion of land from wheat fields into pasturage is an example of factor substitution, and many others could be cited. In agriculture, the purchase of oxen to aid the peasant in plowing and to increase his supply of fertilizer enabled him to work more productively. According to Matteo Villani, Tuscan peasants would not accept a lease unless the landlord provided oxen and seed—in other words, increased capital. In the urban economy, the substitution of capital for labor meant the purchase of better tools or machines—devices that enabled the artisan to work more efficiently. Frequently too, the policy of factor substitution involved technological innovation, the development of entirely new tools and machines. High labor costs promised big rewards to the inventors of labor-saving devices. Chiefly for this reason, the late Middle Ages were a period of impressive technological achievement.

New methods of reproducing the written word offer a clear instance of capital replacing labor by virtue of technology. The growth of universities in the twelfth and thirteenth centuries and the expanding numbers of literate laymen generated a strong demand for books. Numerous scribes were employed to copy manuscripts. At Paris, for example, in the thirteenth century, manuscripts were divided into quires and given to separate scribes, who assiduously reproduced them. The parts were then combined into the finished book. As long as wages were low, this method of reproduction based on intensive human labor was satisfactory enough.

But the late medieval population plunge raised labor costs, and also raised the premium to be claimed by the one who could devise a cheaper way of reproducing books. Johann Gutenberg's invention of printing on the basis of movable metal type in 1453 was only the culmination of many experiments carried on across the previous century. His genius was in finding a way to combine several technologies into the new art. His family had long been associated with the mint of his native city of Mainz, and from this he gained familiarity with presses. He also was an engraver, and he needed that skill to cut the matrices for casting the type. He had to know metallurgy as well, and he successfully combined lead, tin, and antimony into an alloy that melted at low temperature, cast well, and remained strong in the press. Finally, he and all the early printers were businessmen. Printing shops required considerable capital to set up their presses and to market their books. But they were able to multiply texts with unprecedented accuracy and speed, and at greatly reduced costs. The advent of printing is thus a salient example of the policy of factor substitution which was transforming the late medieval economy.[18]

There are many other examples. There occurred a revolution in maritime transport. Its thrust was to produce bigger ships with smaller crews, able to remain long at sea and to sail directly from port to port. Here too, several new technologies affecting both ship construction and the navigational arts were combined to achieve this change. Capital was required as well, and also new business institutions, such as maritime insurance, to encourage and protect the big investments. Even firearms, another innovative technology of the age, can be interpreted in these terms. Soldiers too were commanding higher wages in depopulated Europe, and soldiers with firearms could fight more effectively than those without.

A more diversified economy, a more intensive use of capital, a more powerful technology, and a higher standard of living for the people—these seem the salient characteristics of the late medieval economy, after it recovered from the plague's initial shock and learned to cope with the problems raised by diminished numbers. Specific changes in technology are of course primarily attributable to the inventive genius of individuals. But the huge losses caused by plague and the high cost of labor were the challenge to which these efforts responded. Plague, in sum, broke the Malthusian deadlock of the thirteenth century, which threatened to hold Europe in its traditional ways for the indefinite future. The Black Death devastated society, but it did not cripple human resilience.

Another set of institutions and practices reformed in the wake of the epidemics was the demographic system. To examine the changes in the European demographic system across the late Middle Ages requires first that we understand the principles that govern demographic systems of any sort. People are born and people die, and these events affect the size of the community. But the size of the community also affects these events, through a kind of feedback mechanism, in the language of contemporary systems analysis. Many observers in both the ancient world and the Middle Ages recognized, for example, that the earth could not support infinite human numbers; when overburdened, it periodically purged itself of excess, through famines, wars, plagues, floods, earthquakes, and other natural disasters.[19]

It remained, however, for Thomas Malthus to interpret the relation of community size to vital events in terms of an overarching system. Populations, he argued, inevitably grow faster than their supplies of food, the former tending to increase geometrically, the latter only arithmetically. Predictably, the population would at some point surpass the numbers that its resources could adequately feed. It would then face a reckoning. The reckoning took the form of famines, malnutrition, plagues, and wars, which raised the death rate to a level higher than the birth rate, and thus cut down the size of the community. Malthus called the mechanisms by which growth was restrained and reversed "checks." Those which operated directly on the death rate he named "positive checks." In the world he surveyed, China seemed the land in which the demographic system was most clearly based on the primacy of positive checks. The population repeatedly surged against restraining walls, but death was guarding the ramparts.

Malthus also recognized another type of check that controlled human numbers. These he called "preventive checks."[20] The cost of food, rising as population increased, reduced real wages, as workers had to devote ever greater shares of their disposable income to subsistence. But in some cultures, declining real wages also inhibited marriages, as only those young couples with the means of supporting a family could allow themselves to marry and to set up a new household. In preventing or delaying marriages, this sort of check lowered the birth rate as well. It thus was capable of controlling growth and of keeping the population well within the size its resources could comfortably support. The community need not test the ceiling of subsistence.

Malthus had no way of measuring the true effectiveness of the preventive checks in the Europe he knew as against the positive checks. But recent historians have tried to do so. In particular, in their enterprising survey published in 1981, *The Population History of England*, E. A. Wrigley and Roger Schofield have attempted to estimate not only the total population of England from the sixteenth century to 1871, but also to identify the demographic system or systems which governed its size.[21] They begin their history only in 1541, from which time their principal records, parish registers, survive. They conclude that already in the middle of the sixteenth century preventive checks were more powerful than positive ones in controlling English population. And its relative strength continued to increase in the modern age.

Reliance on preventive rather than positive checks also conferred substantial advantages upon England as presumably upon Europe in early modern times. Controlled population growth meant that increments in output were not immediately consumed in the support of a larger population. Early modern England escaped the Malthusian trap, which kept many nations of the earth on the margins of subsistence and in the grip of poverty. The surpluses that the economy might generate were available for other uses, wise or foolish. Surpluses, allowing for a high rate of reinvestment, were at all events a precondition for eventual industrialization.

Even a superficial reading of modern European history lends these conclusions a certain plausibility. Subsistence crises, famines, even pandemics of the magnitude of the Black Death have not been major factors in modern European history, with the possible exception of the potato blight in Ireland in the 1840s. This suggests that the population contained relatively few persons surviving on the margins of subsistence, who would be the immediate and most likely victims of hunger and disease. Natural disasters of this kind seem strangely tame in Europe in the modern centuries. But if preventive checks were already the principal means of population control in the sixteenth century, then the question at once arises: when, how, and why did it first acquire this predominance?

It is certain that some forms of preventive checks functioned even in the Middle Ages. The chief evidence for this comes from the consistent association in medieval household surveys of wealth and household size. The earliest large survey of a medieval community we possess is the *polyptych* of the abbot Irminon, who presided over the monastery of St. Germain de Près near Paris in the early ninth century.[22] The *polyptych* includes nearly 2,000 entries describing the monastery's possessions in the neighborhood of Paris, some 1,647 of which inventory dependent farms, specify their size, and take note of the serfs and their families who worked and lived on the farms. There are many difficulties with these data, and the survey does not support refined analysis. But if we crudely compare the size of the plowlands, vineyards, and meadows with the number of persons settled upon them, an unmistakable association emerges.[23] Those households with five or fewer units of land show an average size of 3.9 persons; those with six to ten units, 5.43 members; those with 11 to 15, 7.04 members; those with 16 to 20, 8.83; and those with more than 20, 10.07. The progression is clear: the more land, the larger the household living from it.

This close association of extent of land with size of household, evident in our earliest surveys, is very nearly a general rule of household organization in the Middle Ages. It means that the possession of a big farm made possible the support of a big family, but the converse also holds true: those with little land could afford to maintain only small households.

There are many other indications that propertied Europeans in the Middle Ages kept their size of households in balance with their resources. A crucial institution in this regard was the dowry, the contribution that the bride or her family made to the costs of setting up the new household, to what in the Roman legal tradition was called "the burdens of matrimony."[24] In the early Middle Ages the groom or his family had borne the chief burden of these costs, but the flow of property at the making of a marriage changes direction from the twelfth century. The bride's contribution, the true dowry, now predominates.[25] But girls with few resources found it ever more difficult to attract husbands, at least within the propertied classes. A young man too could marry only when able to support a wife. Usually, this meant that he had to wait until he had received the paternal inheritance or had achieved status in a profession or career. Under such conditions, many men married late and some would not marry at all.

Within the propertied classes—chiefly the nobility and the urban patriciate—a linkage was forged between resources and nuptiality, resources and reproduction. What we do not know is whether these restraints affected the behavior of those who owned little or nothing. They are nearly invisible in the sources; our surveys and collections of charters are concerned overwhelmingly with property and the transactions affecting it. The documents ignore the poor. But we do have hints that the poor were very many. The Carolingian capitularies refer to a floating population of drifters and beggars, the *pauperes*.[26] In the early fourteenth century, the chronicler Giovanni Villani tells of a Florentine who bequeathed in his will 6 denarii to "all the poor of Florence, who went about begging."[27] To assure a fair distribution, the executors of the will summoned the poor but locked them up in the biggest parish churches, so that none would receive more than the 6 denarii. Still, the number of poor, both men and women, children and adults, who accepted the donation was more than 17,000. This did not include "the shamefaced poor and those in hospital and prisons and the religious mendicants." They were more than 4,000. Villani was himself astonished by these figures, and thinks that many paupers from outside of Florence must have slipped into the city. On the other hand, these were the ones who supposedly lived by begging. How big would the figure have been, if the needy who did not beg had been included?

Medieval observers shared the view that the poor were much more susceptible than the rich to the ravages of famine and plague. At Florence, Matteo Villani claims that the Black Death of 1348 wiped out the poor completely—those who two decades before were more than 17,000. "And the mendicant poor were almost all dead," he states.[28] "And there were not at that time," he elsewhere observes, any "needy poor."[29]

The presumption that the poor were the chosen victims of hunger and disease persists into early modern times. In the seventeenth century, a Florentine doctor named Alessandro Righi compared the body physical with the body social. The human body was composed of both noble and ignoble parts. The noble parts were the heart, the brain, the liver, and the principal organs. They had the power to expel poisonous substances to the periphery. The ignoble parts, the glands and the skin, had no such powers and thus became the receptacles of the poisons dispatched from the center. So it was with the city. The nobles were the principal organs, and the poor the ignoble skin and glands. "Nor can they," writes the doctor, "transmit [the poison] to others, and therefore it is necessary, that if anything evil is in the city, they receive it and hold it as they are the glands of the city."[30]

The demographic system prevailing in medieval society appears to have been two-tiered. At the bottom of the social ladder, positive checks primarily controlled the numbers of the impoverished. Above this social sector were the middle classes and the wealthy, among whom preventive checks had become the more effective means of regulating numbers. In the Catasto of the city of Florence, dated 1427, wealth shows its characteristic correlation with household size, but, significantly, its influence becomes evident only above a threshold of approximately 400 florins in assessed household wealth.[31] Somewhere between 30 and 40 percent of the households fell below the threshold when wealth began to have a visible influence on household organization and demographic behavior. The demographic system operating in Florence in 1427 still looks to be two-tiered, but now most households had passed under the control of preventive, not positive, checks.

The great population debacle of the late Middle Ages did not, in sum, introduce an entirely new demographic system. But it did redistribute the population between the two tiers of the traditional system. Depopulation gave access to farms and remunerative jobs to a larger percentage of the population. High wages and low rents also raised the standard of living for substantial numbers. They became acquainted with a style of life that they or their children would not want easily to abandon. For a significantly larger part of society, the care of property and the defense of living standards were tightly joined with decisions to marry and to reproduce. Presumably, these are the origins of the demographic system which Wrigley and Schofield find already functioning in sixteenth-century England. Out of the havoc of plague, Europe adopted what can well be called the modern Western mode of demographic behavior.

 THREE

Modes of Thought and Feeling

The impact of the Black Death on the social and cultural life of Europe was similar to its effects upon the economy. Again we must distinguish between what it wrought in the short run, and what in the long. Its chief short-run effect was shock and social fissures, tears in the fabric of society which undermined social discipline and cohesiveness. In the long run, it threatened the quality and continuity of cultural traditions. High mortalities thinned the ranks of the skilled, curtailed the duration of careers, and obstructed recruitment. The result was deterioration, but the decline also stimulated efforts at reform and renewal. In other words, decline was never so deep as to stifle awareness of decline.

We look first at shock and social fissures. The plague caused divisions between the healthy and the sick; between those in the cultural mainstream and those at its margins, namely, strangers, travelers, beggars, lepers, and Jews; and between the mass of society and its cultural leaders, its governors, priests, and physicians. These fissures cut across society in complex and at times pernicious ways, as we shall see.

The shock of plague disrupted the customary ways by which society coped with the passing of its members. Over the centuries the medieval Church had softened the sting of death through comforting rituals. Like last rites in other cultures, their primary purpose was to help the dead achieve eternal rest. But they also instructed the living that the separation was only temporary: on the last day all would be resurrected and reunited. The body too would rise again; even in death it remained a temple of the Holy Spirit and had to be treated with honor. The rituals thus encouraged the living to accept the loss of their loved ones, recruit others to continue the work of the departed, mend the rift in the social fabric that death had caused, and return now to their quotidian labors. Through these rites of passage, not only the dead but the living too were introduced into a new phase of existence. Rituals helped restore mental and social equilibria.

To perform the last rites, the priest came to the bedside of the dying person. He heard a final confession of sins, gave communion, called *viaticum*, "food for a journey," and administered the sacrament of Extreme Unction, the "last anointing." These were largely private rituals. After death, the corpse would be taken by public procession from home to the place of burial. "Outside the house of the dead man," Boccaccio reports, "his friends, neighbors and many others would assemble. Then, according to the status of the deceased, a priest would come with the funeral pomp of candles and chants, while the dead man was borne on the shoulders of his peers to the church chosen before death."[1] The parish church tolled its bells, and sometimes a crier went through the neighborhood to announce the passing. At the church the corpse was blessed; a funeral mass might or might not then be sung. The climax of these last rites was a service at the graveside, in which the priest invoked further blessings upon the deceased. The body was then consigned to holy ground, usually alongside relatives and friends, there in familiar company to await the resurrection. Those in attendance then often partook of a funeral meal—another communion, intended to achieve what the word implies, a reintegration of the community, a healing of the wound that death had inflicted upon it.

According to a recent study of wills from the region of Avignon in southern France, funeral arrangements became ever more elaborate as the fourteenth century progressed.[2] The funerals, at least of the wealthy, developed into veritable "theaters of death." More and more of the people who were making their wills expressed the desire to have a big cortège and to be buried within the parish church itself and not in the outside cemetery—close to the altar and its salvific relics. But even those without the means of securing this privileged space could expect to rest in consecrated earth. They could, that is, if plague permitted.

"As the ferocity of the plague increased," Boccaccio again reports, "such customs ceased either totally or in part, and new ones took their place." It is indeed remarkable how many contemporary observers mention the failure to perform the accustomed rites; they dwell upon the hasty burials of the dead.[3] We return to Boccaccio:

> Now a general procedure was followed more out of fear of contagion than because of charity toward the dead. Alone or with the help of whatever porters they could find, they dragged the corpses from their houses and piled them in front so, particularly in the morning, anyone abroad could see countless bodies. Biers were sent for and when they were lacking, ordinary planks carried the bodies. More than one bier carried two or three together. This happened not just once, but many biers could be counted which held in fact a wife and husband, two or three brothers, or father and son. Countless times, it happened that two priests going forth with a crowd to bury someone were joined by three or four biers carried behind by bearers, so that while the priests thought they had one corpse to bury, they found themselves with six, eight or even more. Nor were these dead honored with tears, candles or mourners. It had come to such a pass that men who died were shown no more concern than dead goats today.[4]

Boccaccio quite rightly attributes this behavior to fear of infection. The cadaver had to be removed as quickly as possible, to a distant burial, in a common ditch, with many other victims. Frequently, lye was sprinkled about the mass graves in order to kill the contagion. Multiple and anonymous burials called into doubt all of the reassuring hope that each body was destined for resurrection. The plague incited a new tension between the living and the dead, even between the living and the sick. Like AIDS victims today, the sick had become the enemy.

A witness at Avignon relates in 1348:

> [Sick] relatives were cared for not otherwise than dogs. They threw them their food and drink by the bed, and then they fled the household. Finally, when they died, strong rustics came from the mountains of Provence, miserable and poor and foul-tempered, who are called gavots. At least, in return for big pay, they carried the dead to burial. No relatives, no friends showed concern for what might be happening. No priest came to hear the confession of the dying, or to administer the sacraments to them. People cared only for their own health [and that of their families]. It even happened that every day a dead rich man was carried to the grave with only a little light and by ruffians—none else followed the corpse but these.[5]

It is of course not true that all families neglected their sick, treating them as if they were not their own, in Boccaccio's phrase. However, even those who tried to nurse sick relatives faced traumatic choices. Boards of Health, set up in the wake of epidemics, were given sweeping powers, which they used to segregate the sick and the suspect from the healthy. By the fifteenth century they characteristically removed those who were infected from their homes and families and consigned them to special, isolated hospitals. Those who entered these pesthouses rarely emerged, and after death would be buried in mass graves, probably in unconsecrated ground, far from ancestors and loved ones. Many families sought to conceal the sickness of a member from the health authorities, although the punishments for so doing were drastic. The administrative records of these Boards of Health include many prosecutions of people who hid from the health authorities the sickness of a household member, or tried to secure a church burial for one who had died of the plague. For even if the family refused to regard a sick member as a menace and an enemy, the Boards of Health had no such qualms.[6] Even the Church had to suspend its normal requirements for Christian burial in periods of plague. *Salus populi suprema lex.*

The fear of the sick and dying easily expanded into a horror of death, into the sense that life itself was a desperate battle against death's dominion. In the thirteenth century, Francis of Assisi had addressed death as a sister. In plague-stricken Europe, death was no longer the kind caretaker of souls awaiting the resurrection. Many historians have noted the changed image of death in late medieval literature and art.[7] It becomes a ravishing monster, the master of a dance in which all must join. One of the great masterpieces of macabre art is the tomb at Avignon of Cardinal La Grange, done shortly before 1400.[8] It shows the cardinal's nearly naked and decomposing body. The inscription reads:

> We are a spectacle to the world. Let the great and humble, by our example, see well to what state they shall be inexorably reduced, whatever their condition, age or sex. Why then, miserable person, are you puffed with pride. Dust you are and unto dust you shall return, rotten corpse, morsel and meal for worms.[9]

Death, as represented in this epitaph, vilified the body; it had become untamed.[10] Revulsion toward death and the dead seemed reflected in the feasts and celebrations that often accompanied epidemics. Boccaccio remarks that during the pestilence, jokes and merrymaking were common at burials.[11] Of course plague mortalities reminded survivors of their own fragile grasp on life, and prompted some of them to spend their remaining hours in revelry. The philosophy appears pedestrian: "eat, drink, and be merry, for tomorrow we die." But the orgies that many witnesses describe seem also the celebration of a victory, however temporary, over death. Why else should a favored site for such behavior be graveyards? At Avignon by the late fourteenth century, the cemetery of Champfleur had become, at least by repute, a place of debauchery. In 1394 a papal official threatened with excommunication those who dared "to dance, fight, throw iron or wooden bars, to play with wheels, to bowl, or play dice or other unseemly games or commit other unseemly acts" over the graves of the dead.[12] Prostitutes solicited in cemeteries, and, by the testimony of contemporaries, fornicators and adulterers trysted among the graves.

The second fissure induced by plague and panic divided those in the cultural mainstream from those at its margins. Relations with strangers, beggars, lepers, Jews, and others were always tense in medieval society, but not usually violent. Jews, for example, the largest cultural minority, long enjoyed the right, recognized by both Roman and canon law, to practice their religion free of interference. But the plague also discredited the leaders of society, its governors, priests, and intellectuals, and the laws and theories supported by them. These elites were obviously failing in their prime social function, the defense of the common welfare, in the name of which they enjoyed their privileges.

Boccaccio points to this breakdown of the old leadership and its rules:

> In this great affliction and misery of our city, the revered authority of both divine and human laws was left to fall and decay by those who administered them. They too, just as other men, were all either dead or sick or so destitute of their families, that they were unable to fulfill any office. As a result, everyone could do just as he pleased.[13]

And Matteo Villani:

> It was thought that the people, whom God by his grace had preserved in life, having seen the extermination of their neighbors and of all the nations of the world . . . would become better, humble, virtuous and catholic, avoiding iniquities and sins and overflowing with love and charity for one another. But . . . the opposite happened. Men, finding themselves few and rich by inheritances and successions of earthly things, forgetting the past as if it never was, gave themselves to the most disordered and sordid behavior than ever before. As they wallowed in idleness, their dissolution led them into the sin of gluttony, into banquets, taverns, delicate foods, and gambling. They rushed headlong into lust. . . . And without any restraint almost all our city took up this shameful style of life; the other cities and provinces of the world did the same or worse.[14]

The terrible violence directed against Jews in 1348 and 1349 was itself a product of these combined rips in the social fabric. Early in 1348, the rumor arose that the Jews of northern Spain and southern France were poisoning the Christian wells, and thus disseminating the plague. Few recognized leaders of medieval society—no emperor, king, or Pope—gave credence to this absurdity. The physician Guy de Chauliac, for example, first mentions the rumor in 1348. The common people, he observed with evident contempt, variously blamed beggars or Jews for the disease's spread. In the same year Pope Clement VI, then at Avignon, tried to discredit the charge in a bull, calling the accusation "unthinkable." After all, he argued, the plague was raging in regions of the world where no Jews were present; and in regions where they resided, they too were its victims. We do not know who launched and sustained the libel; but they were believed, not physicians and popes.

In September and October, at Chinon on Lake Geneva and at Chambéry in the French Alps, formal accusations were brought against Jews for having poisoned the wells. The court officials extracted several confessions, and the rumor spread to the east and north, outracing the spreading epidemic. It next reached Strasbourg in Alsace, from whence it diffused throughout the German lands and passed into Poland.

Riots occurred in Strasbourg, and a government that tried to protect the local Jews was thrown out of office. In this instance too, fear of the plague worked to discredit traditional leadership. With the connivance of the new government, on February 14, 1349, more than 900 Jews, about half the community, were burned on the grounds of the Jewish cemetery. Similar riots and burnings followed in numerous German towns, in the early months of 1349. The fury abated after April, as the old elites with difficulty reestablished order in the towns.

Eliciting the same kind of response in another quarter, the plague undermined confidence in the Church's spiritual leadership. Many spontaneous religious movements arose in the aftermath or even in anticipation of epidemics. Over some the Church was able to maintain an uneasy control, but others mounted a direct challenge to its monopoly over spiritual direction.

Epidemics and the fear of epidemics drove people out on the roads, for which piety provided a ready justification. To go on pilgrimage offered an escape from infected areas and allowed the voyager to visit holy places; the practice benefited both body and soul. There is a paradox here. Plague multiplied the number of people on the highways and byways, but also provoked deep hostility against them, and against all strangers and foreigners. They too, along with other marginal social groups, were under suspicion: they too were at worst the malicious sowers of plague, or at best its unsuspecting carriers. Their ranks, moreover, typically included beggars, thieves, and prostitutes—undesirables who were likely to be the targets of God's wrath wherever they went. Their arrival menaced the community. In periods of plague, towns typically closed their gates to travelers, especially from infested regions, and tried to expel beggars, prostitutes, and other undesirables from their midst.

The problem was aggravated by the very numbers that took to the roads in fear of or in reaction to epidemic. Pope Clement VI, in the plague year of 1348, offered a plenary indulgence to all Christians who repented and confessed their sins. In the same spirit, he declared 1350 to be a year of jubilee, with plenary indulgences for all who visited Rome. Matteo Villani, from his vantage point in Florence, was amazed at the numbers that responded, not only from Italy but from the lands beyond the Alps. "The multitude of Christians [he writes] that went to Rome was impossible to count. By the estimate of those resident in the city, on Christmas day . . . and in Lent up to Easter, the pilgrims to Rome were from one million to 1,200,000. And then from Ascension to Pentecost, more than 800,000. The roads were filled day and night."[15] The heat and the demands for harvest workers, he notes, reduced the numbers to 200,000 during the summer. But never before, he believes, had so many gone on pilgrimage.

Chaucer, in the *Canterbury Tales,* thus portrays a typical medieval practice which fear of illness often inspired. The poet himself mentions that people go to Canterbury in gratitude for cures: "There to the holy sainted martyr kneeling / That in their sickness sent them help and healing."[16] Help and healing: these become the major social concerns in plague-stricken Europe.

Among the most flamboyant of those who seemed to promise help were the flagellants, pilgrims of a special kind. Processions of men through cities, scourging themselves in expiation for their own sins and those of society, were not unprecedented in the history of medieval piety. A similar movement, called the "Great Alleluia," had swept through the cities of Italy in 1260. But the Black Death gave the practice unprecedented dimensions. The flagellants claimed divine authorization for their mission, usually delivered in the form of a letter dropped from heaven. Each band had a leader, but whether any overarching organization joined them all is uncertain. The bands marched from town to town, sleeping outdoors as part of their penance. At the central squares, the leader preached repentance. The marchers sang hymns and performed a kind of ritual dance. At its climax they fell to earth and took positions that indicated the types of sins they had committed—usury, perjury, adultery, murder. They then stripped to the waist and whipped themselves with knotted cords. After this discipline, they donned their clothes and marched on. It was all dramatic theater. But clearly these men seemed to be supplanting the clergy in the role of intermediaries between heaven and earth. This the Church could not allow. In 1348 Pope Clement VI prohibited public flagellation, although the movement was far too powerful and popular to be suppressed.

Flamboyant movements of penance also accompanied the later epidemics. In 1399, for example, a story spread through Italy. In the Dauphiné province in southern France, the Virgin had appeared to a young shepherd. Our Lady told the boy that her divine Son was exasperated by the sins of mankind. He had already in his fury rained death on one-third the human race; what now could dissuade him from its total destruction? Men must do penance and reform. The warning evoked its only recorded response in Italy, but there it was massive. In the summer and fall of 1399, bands of penitents dressed in white marched from city to city singing hymns, doing public penance, and urging peace and reconciliation among warring factions. The great movement of the Bianchi or the Whites occurred a year in advance of a major epidemic, that of 1400, possibly the worst recurrence since 1348. The movement was not initiated by the Church, though the clergy gave it its reluctant blessing. New leaders, unfortunately unknown to us, were guiding and inspiring the faithful.

Is it possible to see here a parallel in the medieval reaction to plague and contemporary fears about AIDS? Many persons today do not believe what the experts relate about AIDS and its modes of transmission. They still want infected children taken from schools, and contacts with the sick severely limited. We seem to witness here too a crisis of confidence in expert opinion, much like the one that occurred in the Middle Ages.

In the long term too, plagues undermined the stability of European culture. Continuing high mortalities thinned the ranks of the skilled and the learned and debased the quality of cultural expressions of every sort. Europe faced the formidable task of maintaining and repairing its cultural heritage.

The crisis had a visible impact upon institutions of education, most notably the universities. The universities trained the theologians, the lawyers, and the academic doctors, the physicians. The plagues cut down the number of students as much as they depleted all other social groups. The enrolled students at Oxford declined in the late fourteenth century from a pre-plague high of some 30,000 to 6,000. A contemporary, John Wyclif, later condemned as a heretic, thought the losses were even greater; he set the numbers falling from a fabulous 60,000 to fewer than 3,000. In all Europe, the number of universities numbered about 30 before 1348; five of these were wiped out completely.[17]

But the epoch of epidemics also witnessed a plethora of new foundations, of both colleges and universities. There were several reasons for this expansion of institutions amidst collapsing human numbers. The depletion of the ranks of the clergy gave deep concern, and the universities were the ones that supplied the leading clerics. Travel was, as we have mentioned, regarded as dangerous, and a local university saved the students from the risks of long journeys to distant schools. Finally, the many deaths produced a great flood of pious bequests, and many of those benefited poor scholars, future priests, and the institutions that trained them.

Thus Cambridge University acquired four new colleges, the

foundations of which can be associated with the Black Death. Gonville was established between 1348 and 1351; Trinity Hall, in 1350; Corpus Christi, in 1352; and Clare Hall, in 1362. Oxford acquired two new colleges: Canterbury, in 1362, and New College, 1372. Even more dramatic was the proliferation of new universities on the Continent. In 1348, Emperor Charles IV, expressing concern for the decay of learning, granted a charter to the new University of Prague, which still today bears his name. It attracted many Czech and German students, who formerly had to travel to Bologna or Paris. Universities were established at Vienna and Cracow in 1364; at Fünfkirchen in Hungary in 1367; and at Heidelberg in 1385. In sum, all the universities east of the Rhine and north of the Alps were founded after the onslaught of epidemics. Most of the authorizing charters mention the shortage of priests and the decay of learning as the reasons for their foundation.

It is interesting to speculate on the cultural results of this proliferation of universities. For one, it undercut the dominance of the older great centers, notably Paris and Bologna. It is hard to evaluate the quality of learning in the new schools, but they probably helped give late scholastic thought its reputation for logic-chopping and futility. They also freed the curriculum of the weight of traditional subjects. At the University of Florence, for example, which was also founded in 1350 in the immediate wake of plague, rhetoric and soon the study of Greek replaced logic at the core of the program in liberal arts. The reform spread quickly to the other universities of Italy and gave a major thrust to the revival of classical studies.

While it weakened the dominance of a few international centers, the proliferation of universities gave the new foundations much more of a national constituency than any school had shown before. This surely loosened the international cohesion of medieval culture and prepared the way for the theological schisms coming in, and even before, the Reformation. The plague helped bring the age of cultural nationalism to Europe.

This trend toward national cultures is seen too in its effects upon the forms of linguistic expression. The number of teachers who knew Latin declined, and this made necessary the use of the vernacular tongues in instruction, at least below the university level. But the bad quality of university Latin provoked a movement too in the opposite direction, initially in Italy: an effort to restore the language not to its medieval but to its classical purity. The Renaissance of classical Latin thus was a counterpoise to the simultaneous emphasis upon vernacular usage.

To evaluate the influence of plague on the bodies of medieval learning is necessarily to indulge in speculation. But some comment can be offered. Medicine is the domain of formal learning most deeply affected. The corps of medical practitioners in medieval society had been deeply divided into four groups: physicians, who held university degrees and knew medical theory but played a limited role in the care of the sick; surgeons, who learned their skills as apprentices and were the most important among those who cared for the sick; barbers, competent to do minor surgery, blood-letting and the like; and practitioners of folk medicine, a group in which women seemingly predominated.

The universities taught the principles of Galenic medicine inherited from the ancient world and received primarily through the mediation of the Arabs. Disease was a disturbance in the balance of the four humors. Galenic medicine had no clear theory of contagion.[18] But observers of the Black Death had no doubt of its contagious nature. Confidence diminished in the assumption that the ancients had said it all. In 1377, the town of Ragusa (present-day Dubrovnik) required that arriving ships, their crews, passengers, and cargoes, be kept for a certain time in isolation, to make sure that plague was not traveling with them. This was the origin of what came to be known as the quarantine. The name is

Venetian, but sooner or later all Europe's ports adopted similar measures. No one now was doubting that plague was contagious.

Several results followed in the field of medical science. On a social level, the challenge of plague broke down the division between theorizing physicians and practicing surgeons, lent new prestige to the surgeons, and gave new impetus to the direct study of the human body in sickness and in health. Anatomical investigations, which had begun before the plague, were now pursued with more urgency and with higher levels of support from public authorities. And, as a more far-reaching consequence, the experience of plague at least began the long, slow reevaluation of the Galenic system leading to the formation of modern pathological theory. The first to advance systematically the theory of contagion was Giovanni Fracastoro (1483–1533), a physician who served as a public health official and who had earlier written an elegant Latin poem about syphilis, giving that new disease its classical-sounding name. The road to modern medicine had scarcely been entered, but the first steps were taken.[19]

In philosophy, the major trend in late medieval schools was a critical attack upon the great philosophical systems developed in the immediate pre-plague period. Thomas Aquinas, who died in 1274, can here serve as an example. This great Dominican had argued that the universe possessed an underlying order, and that the human intellect could achieve at least a partial understanding of its structure. His late medieval critics, called conventionally nominalists, claimed that he was wrong on both counts. The human intellect had not the power to penetrate the metaphysical structures of the universe. It could do no more than observe events as they flowed. Moreover, the omnipotent power of God meant in the last analysis that there could be no fixed natural order. God could change what He wanted, when He wanted. The nominalists looked on a universe dominated by arbitrary motions. Aquinas's sublime sense of order was hard to reconcile with the experience of plague—unpredictable in its appearances and course, unknowable in its origins, yet destructive in its impact. The nominalist argument was consonant with the disordered experiences of late medieval life.

Finally, we consider how plague affected the religious sensibilities of the Middle Ages, not on the level of formal theology but in the beliefs and practices of the people. The entire issue —how Christian were the Middle Ages?—has elicited much scholarly debate. The French historian Jean Delumeau has been especially forceful in arguing that during the medieval centuries only the clergy and a small lay elite practiced a recognizable Christianity; the masses, especially in the countryside, remained ignorant of the principal tenets of the Christian faith.[20] They adhered to a kind of folk paganism only superficially touched by Christian beliefs. Jacques Le Goff advances a similar argument. "At about 1500," he has written, "Christendom was almost a missionary country."[21]

It is, to be sure, not easy to evaluate the religious beliefs of the unlettered masses. How can the historian know the prayers and pieties of people who did not write and who were largely ignored by the book-producing elites? One precious clue which we shall utilize here is naming conventions, what names people gave to their children. The choice of names, presumably made in freedom, is a cultural statement. In choosing a name, parents may evoke the memory of an ancestor or of a renowned hero. They may express good wishes for their offspring, as in the Italian "Dietiguardi," "May God guard you." And they may also invoke for their child a spiritual patron, a saint, a kind of celestial godparent who would look after their baby's welfare. This last choice interests us primarily. It speaks to the awareness that medieval people had of the Christian cult of saints, and also to the importance they attached to the appointment of a spiritual patron. And even the choice of a spiritual patron tells us something of their concerns.

The cult of saints is of course very old, going back to the commemoration of martyrs in the early Church. It is, however, also true that comparatively few medieval people bore a saint's name until quite late in the epoch—a fact that lends support to the thesis that official Christianity was little practiced by the masses. For example, the great ninth-century survey of the abbey of St.-Germain de Près near Paris gives 6,046 male names and 4,036 female names.[22] Most of the persons named were legally "the men of St. Germain," but how many bore the name of the saint, once the bishop of Paris? Only ten of the 6,000 men. Names with a Biblical or Christian association are very rare. Iacobus, Jacques or James, appears only three times, and Iohannes or John, 24. One of the most renowned saints of this place and period was Martin of Tours, a former soldier and hermit. According to his famous legend, he once divided his cloak with a beggar; that night, in his dream, Christ appeared to thank him for it. The cloak was kept as the most precious relic of the Frankish kings; our word, chapel, derives from it. How many men of St. Germain bore the name Martin? Only 31. So it is also among the women; only two carry the name of Geneviève, the saint who saved Paris from the Huns. There are 19 Marys. Among both men and women, names formed from Germanic roots and showing no religious associations hold an overwhelming preponderance. Those with the initial element of "Erme," as in Ermenarius among the men and Ermengardis among the women, number 223 and 178 respectively for the two sexes. The peasants of St.-Germain were not inclined to appoint celestial patrons for their children.

This was of course before the great efflorescence of medieval culture in the twelfth and thirteenth centuries, but even then medieval names show comparatively little religious influence. We can illustrate naming conventions in the thirteenth century, and subsequent changes in them, specifically for the city of Florence. Florentine sources are exceptionally abundant, and the city is attractive too by virtue of its cultural prominence.

In 1260, the commune of Florence summoned its male citizens to march against Siena, and its officials recorded the names of those mustered into the communal army. Their records have partially survived, and are gathered into a collection named after the valley where the battle was fought, the *Libro di Montaperti*. A Swedish scholar, Olof Brattö, studied these names, and I follow his principal conclusions here.[23] He counted up 6,207 persons, bearing some 3,000 names. The stock of thirteenth-century Florentine names was thus very big. Brattö initially selected for special attention 203 names that appeared more than five times; they are shared by 80 percent of the population. By my own calculations, if we rearrange the names by frequency of appearance, then we must count as many as 73 most common names before we can cover one-half the army. In other words, by 1260 Florentines made use of a large variety of names. And the number of names with religious associations is tiny—by Brattö's count; 19.4 percent, about one in five. The two largest categories of names are historical names, like Guido or Aldobrando, with a long tradition at Florence, and augurative names, like Bonaventure or Dietisavli. Nearly 60 percent of the army bear names out of these two categories.

If we take a closer look at the twenty most common names at Florence in 1260, the first place, based on 163 appearances, is held by Iacopo.[24] This is a religious name, and its popularity may reflect the prestige of the church of St. Iacopo di Compostella in Spain, which attracted many Tuscan pilgrims. Third place also goes to a religious name, Giovanni, presumably recalling Florence's own patron saint. But only two others among the twenty have religious associations—Filippo in thirteenth position and Bernardo in fourteenth. The situation is closely analogous in the countryside.[25] With celestial patrons associated with only one out of five Florentine males, it does not appear that the cult of saints had much appeal in the city or the countryside even as late as 1260.

But a dramatic change occurred over the immediately following generations, amounting to a veritable revolution in the choice of Florentine names. To illustrate the shifting choices, we next look at the names of citizens interred at the Dominican convent of Santa Maria Novella, as recorded in a necrology kept by the friars. The males buried between 1290, the date of the earliest entry, and 1350, number only 369, and the distribution is concentrated in the later decades of this period. The women buried were 245. Those interred at Santa Maria Novella represent a richer tier of citizens than the soldiers of 1260, but this affects only marginally the choice of names.[26]

Men's names are noticeably fewer and repetition of them greater. In 1260, as many as 73 names were needed to cover one-half the population. Among the dead males at Santa Maria Novella, this number falls to 27. Likewise, the most popular choices have changed. Of the twenty most common names in 1260, only five are still found in that category in 1290–1350. They are Giovanni, now holding first position; Iacopo, reduced to third; Filippo, advancing from thirteenth to eighth; and Bernardo, falling from fourteenth to nineteenth. Significantly, four of the five survivors are religious names; only Neri in twelfth place is not. They are joined in the top twenty by other religious names: Piero, who had not registered even five appearances in 1260; Francesco, altogether missing from the earlier survey; Andrea, which previously had been far back in the count, in sixty-eighth position. Among the top twenty, names associated with a saint show an increase from four in 1260 to 13 in the pre-plague generation.

Among the women's names, the first position is shared by a religious name, Giovanna, and by one that is not, Lapa, both with 15 appearances. Of the top twenty feminine names, only five are religious. This suggests that the Christianization of Florentine names proceeded more slowly for women than for men, but the direction of evolution was the same.

If the cult of saints is any measure, religious awareness grew more intensive within the Florentine population between the late thirteenth and the middle fourteenth century. The chief disseminators of the new consciousness were doubtlessly the mendicants, especially the Franciscan and Dominican friars. They took as their chief mission the evangelization of the masses. Thus Franciscan influence is unmistakable in the unprecedented popularity of the name Francesco. Rarely encountered in the thirteenth century, it achieves fourth place among the men buried at Santa Maria Novella, even though the convent was Dominican. By the last half of the fifteenth century, it supplants even Giovanni as the most popular Florentine name.[27] Domenico gains too, rising from twenty-second position to as high as tenth in the late fifteenth century, but St. Dominic never equalled the appeal of the little poor man of Assisi, at least within the city.

How did the experience of epidemic affect the choice of names? Quite clearly, the increase in the stock of religious names, and perhaps also the conversion of the Florentine population to intensified religious fervor, had made substantial advances even before the plague appeared. But the Black Death added momentum to the process and profoundly influenced the choice of patrons.[28]

The 1427 Catasto provides the names of all the household heads in Florence—8,372 males and 1,280 women. Now it is only fourteen names that cover half the population, as opposed to 27 in the generation before the plague. The substantial reduction in the stock of names necessarily led to the greater use of family names, to identify individuals.

The names registered in the Catasto show several new choices which can be reasonably attributed to the experience of plague. The most prominent is Antonio, which gained second position after Giovanni in 1427. The name does not appear among the soldiers of 1260, nor among the men buried at Santa Maria

Novella before 1350. Its popularity comes with the great epidemics. In most instances it doubtlessly honors Anthony of Padua, one of the followers of St. Francis, who acquired renown as a preacher and worker of miracles. St. Bernardine of Siena, a contemporary of the Catasto, remarks about him: "God gives to certain saints particular powers of patronage in particular causes, as to St. Anthony of Padua, by whose patronage every day graces and miracles are obtained."[29] Anthony was the special patron of those struck by fever. The name Niccolò too, unknown among the soldiers of 1260 though already present among those interred at Santa Maria Novella, achieves exceptional popularity in the late fourteenth century. It ranks seventh among the Florentine household heads in 1427. It probably recalls the name of another wonderworker, Nicholas of Tolentino, dead in 1320.

Another new name, ranking sixth in 1427, is Bartolomeo, which supplants its hypocoristic Bartolo, a popular name before the plague. Why Bartolomeo should replace Bartolo is not clear, but Bartolomeo is recognizably the name of an apostle. According to his legend, Bartolomeo was flayed and crucified. In the painting of the Last Judgment in the Sistine Chapel, Michelangelo depicted him holding his own skin. As the sign of plague was most manifest on the skin, he too might have some association with the disease. As one who endured dreadful tortures, he knew what pain was like and was a prominent member of the Christian community of sufferers. This perhaps explains his popularity amid raging epidemics.

Still another name that comes to common use in the period of plague is Lorenzo. Deacon of the Church of Rome, he also suffered a painful martyrdom: he was roasted on a gridiron. Like Bartolomeo, he too understood suffering, and would protect his followers from the pains he had known.

Christopher is another new name, not used before the plague. Christopher guarded against sudden death, and death that overtook a person before he or she could receive the sacrament of penance. Given the violence of plagues, his special services were valued. The saint with particular association with plague was Sebastian, a Roman soldier under Emperor Dicoletian who, for reason of his faith, was shot through with arrows. The flying arrow was a traditional symbol of the flight of infection, and the arrow wound resembled plague boils. Like other suffering saints, Sebastian was qualified to ward off the very ills that he had endured. At Florence, however, he is late in appearing; not until after 1450 does his name, in the form of Bastiano, become reasonably common.[30] Two other saints with concern for the sick are Cosmas and Damian, with the former much more popular at Florence than the latter. They are the patrons of physicians. And Cosmas, in the form of Cosimo, was the name of the member of the Medici house who, in 1434, established the family's hegemony over Florence.

The expanding and intensified search for spiritual patrons who knew suffering and had the power to offer help to those stricken by it thus singled out several ancient saints for special veneration. The quest also raised out of obscurity more recent figures. One was Rose of Viterbo, who died about 1250, but acquired stature in her native city only with the plague of 1450.[31] Her frequent intercession on behalf of those infected led the commune to petition the Pope for her formal canonization. Another example comes from Sicily: St. Rosalia, who died about 1160, lived as an anchoress in a grotto near the city of Palermo. The true story of her life is even more obscure than Rose's own, and in her case it was a late plague, that of 1624, which won her prominence at Palermo.[32] At Florence, the plague of 1630 also rendered popular the cult of a saint who died in 1553. This was Domenica da Paradiso. These women saints, elevated by plague to the stature of major intercessors, usually worked their miracles through some sort of physical object—water, bread, or a garment—which was associated with their bodies and was taken to the sick.[33] Women nurses or relatives were often the ones who recommended these procedures. The curative powers of women working through women may reflect the role which they held in the practice of folk medicine, with which these miraculous cures seem closely associated.

But the chief of the plague saints was a man, though it is not sure whether he really existed. This was St. Rock. He was supposedly born about 1295 at Montpellier, where his father was ruler of the town. The infant bore a red cross on his breast, and on Wednesdays and Fridays refused to nurse more than once a day in honor of the Virgin. As a young man, he distributed his wealth among the poor and embarked on a pilgrimage to Rome. The plague was raging in many places on his journey, but he cured the buboes by his touch. He contracted the plague himself at Piacenza and was expelled from the town. He returned to Montpellier, where he was imprisoned as a spy; he died there in 1327—well before the plague had actually entered Europe. He seems to have gained his reputation as healer in 1414, when he was credited with saving the Council of Constance from infection. Late in the century, a Venetian humanist and governor of Brescia named Francesco Diedo wrote down his legend. Iconographically, St. Rock is presented with his pilgrim staff and purse, and often with a dog; he points to a plague boil on his inner thigh.[34]

The frantic search for celestial protection affected other religious practices. Princes and the wealthy amassed treasuries of relics, which they hoped would guard their health. In their wills they called for Masses to be sung for their souls in what seems preposterous numbers—sometimes in the thousands, as if heaven could be forced open if enough Masses were piled up at the gates. French scholar Jacques Chiffoleau calls this mania for numbers "heavenly accounting."[35] He associates this quantitative bent with the emergence of the calculating mind of the modern world. The argument is not altogether convincing. But there is no doubt that fear of an untimely death profoundly affected the practices and style of late medieval religious life.

Europe at about 1300 was a land caught in a Malthusian deadlock, in a demographic and economic situation which paralyzed its capacity to improve the ways it produced its goods. That system, marked by saturated use of resources and stagnant outputs, might have persisted indefinitely. The plague broke the deadlock, and allowed Europeans to rebuild their demographic and economic systems in ways more admissive of further development. Culturally, the plague thinned the cadres of the skilled and learned and reduced their years of service; it weakened schools and universities; and it compromised the quality of cultural traditions. But it also prepared the road to renewal. Moreover, the fear of plague and of unforeseen death intensified the religious consciousness of the population and disseminated it across larger sectors of society. But it also favored the development of a kind of medicinal, even magical religion, the chief feature of which was the cult of protector and healer saints. To many, particularly among the educated, the cult of saints, their relics and shrines, had seemed superstitious or idolatrous. The saints were usurping the veneration due to God alone. The plague and the style of piety it promoted set the stage for a protracted and divisive debate over the nature of pure religion. The sounds of religious dispute echo down the centuries of the late Middle Ages and the early modern epoch. And the debate helped provoke eventual schism in the Christian community. Europe proved to be a strong patient, and emerged from its long bout with pestilence healthier, more energetic, and more creative than before.[36] But its civilization has not outlived all the *sequelae* of the great epidemics.

Notes

I have made only minor adjustments to the text of David Herlihy's lectures. His notes, however, were incomplete. In revising them, I have confined my commentary largely to my introduction.

Introduction

1. David Herlihy, *Pisa in the Early Renaissance: A Study of Urban Growth* (New Haven: Yale University Press, 1958).
2. These have been collected in Herlihy, *The Social History of Italy and Western Europe, 700–1200* (London: Variorum Reprints, 1978).
3. See Herlihy, *Medieval and Renaissance Pistoia: The Social History of an Italian Town, 1200–1430* (New Haven: Yale University Press, 1967), esp., pp. 102–120; Herlihy, "A Spectral Analysis of Deaths in Florence, 1275–1500," written with the assistance of Perry Gluckman and Mary Pori, both of whom were at the Center for Advanced Study in the Behavioral Sciences of Stanford University, where Herlihy was in residence during the academic year 1972–73. Herlihy and Christiane Klapisch-Zuber, *Les Toscans et leurs familles: Une étude du catasto de 1427* (Paris: Fondation Nationale des Sciences Politiques/Ecole des Hautes Etudes en Sciences Sociales, 1978), p. 194, briefly summarize the results from this study. It is cited as "Typescript. Center for Advanced Study in the Behavioral Sciences, 1973."

4. Herlihy, *Pistoia,* pp. 65–66.
5. Emmanuel Le Roy Ladurie, *Les paysans de Languedoc,* 2 vols. (Paris: Imprimerie Nationale, 1966), and M. M. Postan, *Essays on Medieval Agriculture and General Problems of the Medieval Economy* (Cambridge: Cambridge University Press, 1973).
6. Herlihy, *Pistoia,* p. 117. More recently, John Hatcher, in his *Plague, Population and the English Economy 1348–1530* (London: Macmillan, 1977), has argued against this interpretation, emphasizing once again mortality as the key demographic variable for understanding the stagnation of Europe's population through much of the fifteenth century. For a contrary view, see Larry Poos, *A Rural Society after the Black Death: Essex 1350–1525* (Cambridge: Cambridge University Press, 1991), pp. 121–129; and Jim Bolton, " 'The World Upside Down': Plague as an Agent of Economic and Social Change," in *The Black Death in England,* ed. by Mark Ormrod and Phillip Lindley (Stamford: Paul Watkins, 1996), pp. 39–40.
7. "Spectral Analysis," 17–18.
8. For this distinction, see Chapter 2 above and the excellent discussions of Pier Paolo Viazzo, *Upland Communities: Environment, Population and Social Structure in the Alps since the Sixteenth Century* (Cambridge: Cambridge University Press, 1989), pp. 7, 42–46, 178–179. See also Herlihy and Klapisch-Zuber, *Les Toscans et leurs familles,* pp. 209–214.
9. Herlihy, *Pistoia,* p. 145; and "Population, Plague and Social Change," p. 242.
10. Herlihy begins "Population, Plague and Social Change in Rural Pistoia" with criticisms of Enrico Fiumi's interpretation of the plague's role in late medieval social and economic history: "His silence implies that he holds the plagues, famines and accompanying demographic decline of the fourteenth century to be fortuitous interventions, pure acts of God, to which no social or economic factor substantially contributed" (p. 226).
11. Barbara F. Harvey, "Introduction: The 'Crisis' of the Early Fourteenth Century," in *Before the Black Death: Studies in the 'Crisis' of the Early Fourteenth Century,* ed. by Bruce M. S. Campbell (Manchester: University of Manchester Press, 1991), pp. 1–24, has

recently reached a similar conclusion: "Left to its own devices, the early fourteenth-century economy would not have proved capable of fundamental long-term changes, comparable to those which actually took place in the very different circumstances created by the Black Death. . . . it was in fact the advent of plague, an exogenous factor, that transformed the economic life of Western Europe in the later Middle Ages, and the changes which actually occurred after that event could not have been predicted in the first half of the century."

12. See the special number of the *Journal of Interdisciplinary History,* 14, 2 (1983): 199–534: *Hunger and History: The Impact of Changing Food Production and Consumption Patterns on Society;* and in particular Massimo Livi-Bacci, "The Nutrition-Mortality Link in Past Times: A Comment," pp. 293–298; and his later book, *Population and Nutrition: An Essay on European Demographic History* (Cambridge: Cambridge University Press, 1991 [Bologna: Il Mulino, 1987]). See also John Walter and Roger Schofield, "Famine, Disease and Crisis: Mortality in Early Modern Society," in *Famine, Disease and Social Order in Early Modern Society,* ed. by Walter and Schofield (Cambridge: Cambridge University Press, 1989), pp. 1–73, esp. pp. 18–21.

13. Campbell, "Population Pressure, Inheritance, and the Land Market in a Fourteenth-Century Peasant Community," pp. 87–135, in *Land, Kinship and Life-Cycle,* ed. by Richard M. Smith (Cambridge: Cambridge University Press, 1984), especially pp. 120, 127.

14. According to a keyword search for "Black Death," "pest," "plague," and "peste" in the British Library catalogue, Herlihy's claims for the late 1970s and early 1980s seem justified. After 1985 to 1995, however, the number of titles with these words has declined markedly. Nonetheless, since Herlihy's lectures of 1985 several important works have appeared, especially about German-speaking and Nordic countries—areas that received scant attention in Herlihy's essays. For a review of that literature as of 1979, see Neithard Bulst, "Der Schwarze Tod: Demographische, wirtschafts-und kulturgeschichtliche Aspekte der Pestkatastrophe von 1347–1352. Bilanz der neueren Forschung," *Saeculum,* 30 (1979): 45–67.

Among the recent books and articles that have appeared after Herlihy's lectures, see Hatcher, "England in the Aftermath of the Black Death," *Past & Present*, 144 (1994): 3–35; Poos, *A Rural Society after the Black Death; Die Pest 1348 in Italien: Fünfzig zeitgenössische Quellen*, ed. by Klaus Bergdolt (Heidelberg: Manutius Verlag, 1989); William B. Ober, "The Plague at Granada, 1348–49: Ibn al-Khatib and Ideas of Contagion," in *Bottoms up! A Pathologist's Essays on Medicine and the Humanities* (Carbondale: University of Southern Illinois Press, 1987), pp. 288–294; *Manchester Medieval Source Series: The Black Death*, trans. and ed. by Rosemary Horrox (Manchester: Manchester University Press, 1994); *La pesta nera: Dati di una realtà ed elementi di una interpretazione*. Atti del XXX Convegno storico internazionale, Todi, 10–13 ottobre 1993 (Spoleto: Centro Italiano di Studi sull'Alto Medioevo, 1994); František Graus, *Pest, Geissler, Judenmorde: Das 14. Jahrhundert als Krisenzeit* (Göttingen: Vandenhoek & Ruprecht, 1987); Karl Georg Zinn, *Kanonen und Pest: über die Ursprünge der Neuzeit im 14. und 15. Jahrhundert* (Ophalen: Westdeutscher Verlag, 1989); *Before the Black Death: Studies in the 'Crisis' of the Early Fourteenth Century*, ed. by Bruce Campbell (Manchester: Manchester University Press, 1991); Helde Schmölzer, *Die Pest in Wien* (Vienna: Osterreichischer Bundesverlag, 1988); Ole Jorgen Benedictow, *Plague in the Late Medieval Nordic Countries: Epidemiological Studies* (Oslo: Middelalderforlaget, 1992); Neithard Bulst, "Krankheit und Gesellschaft in der Vormoderne: Das Beispiel der Pest," in *Maladies et société (XIIe-XVIIIe siècles)*, ed. by Bulst and Robert Delort. Actes du colloque de Bielefeld, novembre 1986 (Paris: Editions du Centre National de la Recherche Scientifique, 1989), pp. 17–55; *The Black Death in England*, ed. by Ormrod and Lindley.

15. See Ann Carmichael, "Infection, Hidden Hunger, and History," *Journal of Interdisciplinary History*, 14, 2 (1983): 261.

16. See Anna Lucia Forti Messina, "L'Italia dell'Ottocento di fronte al colera," in *Storia d'Italia: Annali 7: Malattia e medicina*, ed. by Franco Della Peruta (Turin: Einaudi, 1984), pp. 427–494; and Charles E. Rosenberg, *The Cholera Years: The United States in 1832, 1849, and 1866* (Chicago: University of Chicago Press, 1962), pp. 55–64.

17. Chiara Borro Saporiti, "L'endemia tubercolare nel secolo XIX: Ipotesi per ripensare un mito," in Della Peruta, *Malattia e medicina*, pp. 841–875; and Domenico Preti, "La lotta antitubercolare nell'Italia fascista," in ibid., pp. 953–1015; and Pierre Guillaume, *Du désespoir au salut: Les tuberculeux aux 19e et 20e siècles* (Paris: Aubier, 1986), pp. 131–169.

18. Herlihy also drew parallels between the Black Death and the AIDS virus in "The Black Death: Shock and Social Fissures," *The Maine Scholar*, 5 (1992): 33–44.

19. See Alfred W. Crosby, *Ecological Imperialism: The Biological Expansion of Europe, 900–1900* (Cambridge: Cambridge University Press, 1986); John Henderson, "Epidemics in Renaissance Florence: Medical Theory and Government Response," in *Maladies et société*, pp. 165–188, esp. p. 169; Jon Arrizabalaga, Roger French, and Henderson, eds., *The Great Pox: The French Disease in Renaissance Europe* (New Haven: Yale University Press, 1997); Roger French, "The Arrival of the French Disease in Leipzig," in *Maladies et société*, pp. 133–141; and Anna Foa, "The New and the Old: The Spread of Syphilis (1494–1530)," in *Sex and Gender in Historical Perspective*, ed. by Edward Muir and Guido Ruggiero (Baltimore, Johns Hopkins University Press, 1990), pp. 26–45.

20. According to Messina, "L'Italia dell'Ottocento," p. 431, cholera also struck the public imagination because of its spontaneous appearance and mysterious character. But by the middle of the nineteenth century doctors realized that its cause and cure depended on sanitary conditions and in particular on clean water and the proper disposal of sewage; ibid., p. 436.

21. This is a hypothesis that must be tested with comparative analysis. Messina, "L'Italia dell'Ottocento," pp. 480–481, 489, reports the fears and reactions of the poor against the medical profession and hospitals during the cholera epidemics of the nineteenth century ("veleno! vogliono farci morire, perché siamo troppo"). See also Paolo Sorcinelli, "Uomini ed epidemie nel primo Ottocento: comportamenti, reazioni e paure nello Stato pontificio," in *Malattia e medicina*, pp. 495–537. But neither author concludes that the medical profession declined in respect during the century. Indeed, it was quite the opposite: the nineteenth century saw the rapid spread and legitimization of the medical profession in Italy. According to Ada

Lonni, "Medici, ciarlatani e magistrati nell'Italia liberale," in *Malattia e medicina,* pp. 799–840, a new trust in the ability of doctors to cure disease spread through the Italian population at least in the major cities during the nineteenth century.

On the decline in the status of the medical profession after the Black Death of 1348 and public distrust of it, see Katharine Park, *Doctors and Medicine in Early Renaissance Florence* (Princeton: Princeton University Press, 1985), pp. 34–42, 237–238. For a contemporary source that links the Black Death with the decline in skills and prestige of the medical profession, the clergy, and educators, see William Langland, *Piers the Ploughman,* transl. by J. F. Goodridge (Harmondsworth: Penguin, 1959). Historians have questioned these generalizations, however. William J. Courtenay, "The Effect of the Black Death on English Higher Education," *Speculum,* 55, 4 (1980): 696–714, argues that support and respect for education and educators increased in England after the Black Death through the second half of the fourteenth century. William J. Dohar, *The Black Death and Pastoral Leadership: The Diocese of Hereford in the Fourteenth Century* (Philadelphia: University of Pennsylvania Press, 1995), has emphasized the "heroic efforts of John Trillek" (bishop of Hereford) to ensure that the diocese where Langland lived maintained high levels of recruitment and upheld the standard of priestly qualifications in the post-plague period. Similarly, Christopher Harper-Bill, "The English Church and English Religion after the Black Death," pp. 79–124, in *The Black Death in England,* has claimed: "What is most striking is the consistently high standard of episcopal governance over almost two centuries from the Black Death to the Reformation" (p. 105).

22. At least for Italy, the authors of *Malattia e medicina* do not report any correlations between the outbreak of disease and the search for scapegoats or pogroms against Jews or aliens. Indeed, according to Giorgio Gattai, the spread of syphilis in the nineteenth century promoted the "birth of 'tolerance'." ("La sifilide: Medici e poliziotti interno alla 'Venere politica'," pp. 739–798.) Following the outbreak of cholera in Hamburg in 1892, right-wing politicians were unsuccessful in provoking anti-Jewish violence. Instead, criticism led to social and governmental reform; see Richard J. Evans,

Death in Hamburg: Society and Politics in the Cholera Years 1830–1910 (Oxford: Clarendon Press, 1987), pp. 387–401.

23. See most recently Graus, *Pest, Geissler, Judenmorde*. Plagues in early modern Italy led to the fear and repression of the poor mixed with acts of charity; see Brain Pullan, "Plague and Perceptions of the Poor in Early Modern Italy," in *Epidemics and Ideas: Essays on the Historical Perception of Pestilence*, ed. by Terence Ranger and Paul Slack (Cambridge: Cambridge University Press, 1992), pp. 101–123. Anti-Semitic pogroms did not occur everywhere, however, as historians of Great Britain and Italy are well aware. An atlas analyzing and comparing areas free from post-plague pogroms with those stricken by them is much needed.

24. The essays in Ranger and Slack, eds., *Epidemics and Ideas*, provide a greater sense of the commonalities in the psychological reactions to disease across history than does Herlihy; see in particular Slack, "Introduction," pp. 1–20, esp. pp. 3–5. On the beginnings of a comparative approach to diseases in early modern Europe, see Bulst, "Krankheit und Gesellschaft in der Vormoderne." On Jews, Indians, the French, and lepers as "the Other" sought out for blame with the spread of syphilis, see Foa, "The New and the Old." But in the case of syphilis, Foa concludes that "the idea of contagion, with its totally natural means of transmission, tended to eliminate an essential aspect of blaming: the aura of mystery that always surrounded it" (p. 31). For American hysteria following the outbreak of tuberculosis at the time of World War I and its consequences for class and race hatred, see Katherine Ott, "The Intellectual Origins and Cultural Form of Tuberculosis in the United States, 1870–1925," Ph.D diss., Temple University (1990), pp. 278–285; for France, Guillaume, *Du désespoir au salut*, pp. 81–105. For riots and popular violence in southern Italy after the outbreak of cholera, see Francesco Leoni, *Il Colera nell'Italia meridionale (1836–1837)*, 2nd ed. (Rome: Editrice Apes, 1990); and more generally on fear and its reactions, Sorcinelli, *Nuove epidemie, antiche paure: Uomini e colera nell'Ottocento* (Milan: Franco Angeli, 1986) esp. pp. 32–49; and Rosenberg, *The Cholera Years*, pp. 55–64. On typhus and influenza as "new diseases," see Carmichael, "Infection and Hidden Hunger," pp. 258–261.

25. See J. F. D. Shrewsbury, *A History of Bubonic Plague in the British Isles* (Cambridge: Cambridge University Press, 1970); Graham Twigg, *The Black Death: A Biological Reappraisal* (London: Batsford Academic and Educational, 1984). Also see the work of the physician and historian of medicine, Ann Carmichael, *Plague and the Poor in Renaissance Florence* (Cambridge: Cambridge University Press, 1986), pp. 18–26, who maintains that the plague was accompanied by a variety of other contagious infections: smallpox, influenza, and typhus. On the interaction of diseases in history, see her "Infection and Hidden Hunger."

26. On the supposed ignorance of contemporary observers, see Robert S. Gottfried, *The Black Death: Natural and Human Disaster in Medieval Europe* (London: Hale, 1983; 2nd ed., 1986), p. 110: "But it is surprising that virtually all of the medical observers failed to make the connection between plague and the plethora of dead rodents that preceded an epidemic."

27. See most recently the introduction to the collection of sources on the Black Death edited and translated by Horrox, *The Black Death,* p. 5: "What such writers were describing were quite clearly cases of bubonic and pneumonic plague." Benedictow, *Plague in the Late Medieval Nordic Countries; The Pest Anatomized: Five Centuries of Plague in Western Europe: An Exhibition at the Wellcome Institute for the History of Medicine* (London: The Wellcome Institute, 1985); Gottfried, *The Black Death.* Except for Gottfried's discredited book (see Stuart Jenks's review, *Journal of Economic History,* 46 (1986): 815–823; Caroline Walker Bynum, "Disease and Death in the Middle Ages," *Culture, Medicine and Psychiatry,* 9 (1985): 97–102; and John Norris's review in the *Bulletin of the History of Medicine,* 58 (1984): 250–252), historians have recently eliminated pneumonic plague as the source of the unusually swift contagion. On pneumonic plague, see Shrewsbury, *A History of Bubonic Plague;* Twigg, *The Black Death,* p. 163 and Benedictow, *Plague,* pp. 266–267.

28. I know of few historians other than David Herlihy who have supported the radical claims of Twigg, *The Black Death.* On the basis of the complete absence of contemporary reports of dying rats or other rodents accompanying the plague, average annual tempera-

tures in Great Britain that would not support a rat or flea population required for the mammoth mortalities scored by the plague, and the rapidity of dissemination over long distances wholly incomparable with modern plague even when assisted by steamships and railroads, Twigg argues tentatively for another disease candidate—anthrax. This speculative conclusion put forward in his final chapter is less convincing than the previous ten chapters, which forcefully refute the assumption that the 1348 plague and subsequent waves of fourteenth-century pestilence were bubonic and pneumonic plagues. Reviewers raised the objection that there are no known modern cases in which anthrax has taken on such epidemic propositions. (In Twigg's defense, no epidemics in modern records have reached the levels of the Black Death's mortality relative to population.) But had the plague been anthrax, why were the cattle-grazing regions of Europe the least affected by the Black Death? See Léopold Genicot, "Crisis: From the Middle Ages to Modern Times," *The Cambridge Economic History of Europe*. Vol. I: *The Agrarian Life of the Middle Ages* (2nd ed.), ed. by M. M. Postan (Cambridge: Cambridge University Press, 1966), pp. 660–741.

The anthrax speculation is only a short coda to Twigg's important book. Indeed, in a later article which largely summarizes his book, "The Black Death in England: An Epidemiological Dilemma," in *Maladies et société*, pp. 75–98, Twigg does not even mention anthrax. Instead, he argues: "The logistics of the epidemic in England support the hypothesis of an air-borne organism of high infectivity and virulence, having a short incubation period and being spread by respiratory means" (p. 98).

Despite Twigg's array of overwhelming evidence that the plagues of the mid-fourteenth through fifteenth centuries could not have been bubonic or pneumonic plague, historians in Britain have largely ignored his book, while Americans have rejected its findings out of hand, without any counterarguments. Further, recent works on the fourteenth- and fifteenth-century plagues continue to maintain that the disease was bubonic but with no new evidence or rebuttal to Twigg's argument. See previous note.

29. Guy de Chauliac's contemporary in Avignon, the physician Raymond Chalmel de Viviers, also mentions the "bubo," but it was

only one of the 22 signs of pestilence listed in his *De peste libri tres,* ed. by Robert Hoeniger in *Der schwarze Tod in Deutschland* (Berlin: Grosser, 1882), p. 171. On Gentile da Folgino's *consilia* on the plague and his analysis of "the signs," see Jon Arrizabalaga, "Facing the Black Death: Perceptions and Reactions of University Medical Practitioners," in *Practical Medicine from Salerno to the Black Death,* ed. by L. García-Ballester, R. French, J. Arrizabalaga, and A. Cunningham (Cambridge: Cambridge University Press, 1994), pp. 237–288.

30. E. A. Wrigley and Roger Schofield, *The Population History of England 1541–1871: A Reconstruction* (London: Edward Arnold, 1981). As far as birth control goes, Wrigley has revised his earlier claims based on Colyton. See his "Family Limitation in Pre-Industrial England," *Economic History Review,* 19 (1966): 82–109, and "Marital Fertility in Seventeenth-Century Colyton: A Note," in ibid.: 429–436. Herlihy and Klapisch-Zuber, in *Les Toscans et leurs familles,* pp. 439–446, continued to speculate that birth control was practiced by the Florentine population in the fifteenth century. For a criticism of their argument see Rudolph Binion, "Fiction as Social Fantasy: Europe's Domestic Crisis of 1879–1914," *Journal of Social History,* 27, 4 (1994): 697–698.

31. Huizinga, Johan, *The Autumn of the Middle Ages,* transl. by Rodney Payton and Ulrich Mammitzsch (Chicago: University of Chicago Press, 1996; Dutch orig.; Haarlem, 1919).

32. Millard Meiss, *Painting in Florence and Siena after the Black Death: The Arts, Religion, and Society in the Mid-Fourteenth Century* (Princeton: Princeton University Press, 1951).

33. Alberto Tenenti, *Il senso della morte e l'amore della vita nel Rinascimento (Francia e Italia)* (Turin: Einaudi, 1957); see the review essay by Salvatore Camporeale, "Senso della morte e amore della vita nel Rinascimento: Susone, Valla, Erasmo, e il 'problema della salvezza,' " *Memorie Domenicane,* n.s. 8–9 (1977–78): 439–450.

34. Philippe Ariès, *The Hour of Our Death,* trans. Helen Weaver (London: Allen Lane, 1981).

35. Philip Ziegler, *The Black Death* (London: Collins, 1969); and Gottfried, *The Black Death.*

36. Horrox, *The Black Death,* p. 22. For other examples, see documents

pp. 30, 43, and 69; and Cohn, *Cult of Remembrance and the Black Death: Six Renaissance Cities in Central Italy* (Baltimore: Johns Hopkins University Press, 1992).

37. *Tutte le opere di Giovanni Boccaccio,* ed. Vittore Branca (Milan: Mondadori, 1976), vol. 4, p. 14.

38. *Il Canzoniere,* ed. by Sebastione Blancato (Milan, 1946), p. 129, Sonnet 99: "S'i'fossi."

39. Horrox's translation, *The Black Death,* p. 136; for a slightly different slant, see the Goodridge translation, Langland, *Piers the Ploughman,* p. 62.

40. See Cohn, *Cult of Remembrance.*

41. See Cohn, *Death and Property in Siena: Strategies for the Afterlife* (Baltimore: Johns Hopkins University Press, 1988), and *The Cult of Remembrance.* Philippe Ariès, *L'enfant et la vie familiale sous l'Ancien Régime* (Paris: Plon, 1960), and Lawrence Stone, *The Family, Sex and Marriage in England 1500–1800* (London: Weidenfeld and Nicolson, 1977), have argued that parents did not develop ties of affection with their children until the eighteenth century because earlier high rates of infant and adolescent mortality had blunted these affections. These arguments have come under sharp attack; see for instance David Herlihy, "Medieval Children," in *Essays on Medieval Civilization: The Walter Prescott Webb Memorial Lectures,* ed. by Bede Karl Lackner and Kenneth Roy Philip (Austin: University of Texas Press, 1978), pp. 109–141; Simon Schama, *The Embarrassment of Riches* (New York: Knopf, 1986); Richard Trexler, *Public Life in Renaissance Florence* (New York: Academic Press, 1980). Yet no one has speculated that the very opposite relationship may have been at work, at least for the post-Black Death period, as Langland's verse and the changes in late medieval testaments suggest: plague and high levels of mortality caused parents to spoil their children with excessive affection.

42. These figures come from the *incunabula* database compiled by the British Museum. It is the largest database for early printing anywhere and contains not only the Brtitish Museum's vast holdings of *incunabula* but all known survivals. I wish to thank Martin Davies, curator of the *incunabula* section of the British Library, for his assistance. On the population trends of the late fifteenth century,

Notes to Page 11

see Herlihy, "Deaths, Marriages, Births, and the Tuscan Economy (ca. 1300–1550)," in *Population Patterns in the Past,* ed. by Ronald Demos Lee (New York: Academic Press, 1977), pp. 135–164; Herlihy, "The Population of Verona in the First Century of Venetian Rule," in *Renaissance Venice,* ed. by J. R. Hale (London: Faber, 1973), pp. 91–120; and David Sabean, "German Agrarian Institutions at the Beginning of the Sixteenth Century: Upper Swabia as an Example," in *The German Peasant War of 1525,* ed. by Janos M. Bak (London: Cass, 1976), pp. 78–79.

43. See Alfred Doren, *Studien in der Florentiner Wirtschaftgeschichte,* 2 vols. (Stuttgart: J. G. Cotta'sche Nachfolger, 1901–1908); Bruno Dini, "L'industria serica in Italia. Secc. XIII–XV," in *La seta in Europa. Secc. XIII–XX, Atti della 24a settimana di studi "F. Datini" di Prato,* ed. by S. Cavaiciocchi (Florence: Olschki, 1983); Walter Endrei, *L'évolution des techniques du filage et du tissage de moyen âge à la revolution industrielle,* trans. by Joseph Takacs (Paris: Mouton, 1968), pp. 91–123; Eleanora M. Carus-Wilson, "An Industrial Revolution of the Thirteenth Century" and "The English Cloth Industry in the Late Twelfth and Early Thirteenth Centuries," in *Medieval Merchant Venturers: Collected Studies* (London: Methuen, 1954); and John H. Munro, "Textile Technology," in *Dictionary of the Middle Ages,* ed. Joseph Strayer (New York: Scribner, 1988), vol. 11, pp. 693–711: "The textile technology of the early modern era differed from the medieval only in the improvement and spread of the Saxony spinning wheel, and of fulling and gig mills, and the adoption of waterpowered calendaring machines. None of these changes can compare in their impact on textiles with the medieval innovations in carding, spinning, weaving, and fulling" (p. 709).

44. B. H. Slicher Van Bath, *The Agrarian History of Western Europe, A.D. 500–1850* (London: Edward Arnold, 1963), pp. 170–194: "After the important inventions and improvements in the first half of the Middle Ages, the innovations of the latter half seem comparatively modest." (p. 185) Van Bath finds just the opposite relationship between technological advance and population: it was periods of agricultural booms that stimulated technological change. The classic statement equating periods of technological innovation

94

with demographic decline and scarcity of manpower is Marc Bloch's. He accounts for the diffusion of the water mill during the seventh century in "Avenement et conquètes du moulin à eau," *Annales d'histoire économique et sociale,* 7 (1935); for a critical overview of this demographic explanation for technological advancement, see Carlo M. Cipolla, "Per una storia della produttività nei secoli del medioevo e del rinascimento," in *Produttività e technologie nei secoli XII–XVII,* ed. by S. Mariotti (Florence: Le Monnier, 1981), pp. 3–7.

45. The date of invention or first appearance in the documents of a technology may not be the same as the diffusion of a new agricultural practice. Herlihy, "Santa Maria Impruneta: A Rural Commune in the Late Middle Ages," in *Florentine Studies: Politics and Society in Renaissance Florence,* ed. by Nicolai Rubinstein (London: Faber, 1968), pp. 242–276, argues that despite earlier anticipations, it was well after the Black Death that the *mezzadria* system and new forms of capital investments in the land became diffused in the countryside surrounding Florence.

46. Van Bath, *The Agrarian History,* p. 186.

47. Bruce M. S. Campbell and Mark Overton, "A New Perspective on Medieval and Early Modern Agriculture: Six Centuries of Norfolk Farming c. 1250–c.1850," *Past & Present,* 141 (1993): 38–105, esp. p. 41.

48. Carlo M. Cipolla, *Guns and Sails in the Early Phase of European Expansion 1400–1700* (London: Collins, 1965).

49. The term was coined by Michael Roberts, "The Military Revolution, 1560–1660," An Inaugural Lecture delivered before Queen's University of Belfast (Belfast, 1956). Geoffrey Parker, "The 'Military Revolution'—a Myth?" *Journal of Modern History,* 48 (1976): 195–214; and *The Military Revolution: Military Innovation and the Rise of the West, 1500–1800* (Cambridge: Cambridge University Press, 1988), challenged Roberts's thesis but kept its essential lines of argument, only extending the dates of the Military Revolution to 1530–1730. See Michael Duffy, "Introduction: The Military Revolution and the State 1500–1800," in *The Military Revolution and the State 1500–1800* (Exeter: University of Exeter Press, 1980), pp. 1–10.

50. "The Josephine Waters Bennett Lecture: Tuscan Names, 1200–1530," *Renaissance Quarterly* 41, 4 (1988): 561–583.

51. See especially C. M. de la Roncière, "L'influence des franciscains dans la campagne de Florence au XIVe siècle (1280–1360)," *Mélanges de l'école française de Rome—Moyen Age* 87, 1 (1975): 27–103; and his "Aspects de la religiosité populaire en Toscane: Le contado florentin des années 1300," in *La Toscana nel secolo XIV: Caratteri di una civiltà regionale,* ed. by Sergio Gensini (Pisa: Pacini, 1988), vol. I, pp. 337–384. Similarly, Robert Brentano, *A New World in a Small Place: Church and Religion in the Diocese of Rieti, 1188–1378* (Berkeley: University of California Press, 1994), p. 310, finds that these saints' names are already popular by the end of the thirteenth century.

52. La Roncière, "L'influence des franciscains," p. 33: "Le succès de Francesco est éphémère. Le declin s'amorce peut-être dès avant la peste: la faiblesse du pourcentage des Francesco à S. Appiano chez les survivants de 1348 fait supposer que la flambée allumée en 1315 a cessé avant 1350. La césure de 1348 est en tout cas incontestable dans les quatre cantons cités."

53. Herlihy, "Tuscan Names," p. 579. Curiously, Herlihy makes no mention of la Roncière's earlier arguments, especially in "L'influence des franciscains."

54. Herlihy, "Tuscan Names," p. 576.

55. For a comparative treatment of the religious and psychological effects of the Black Death in Tuscany and Umbria, see Cohn, *The Cult of Remembrance.*

56. *The Brenner Debate: Agrarian Class Structure and Economic Development in Pre-Industrial Europe,* ed. by T. H. Aston and C. H. E. Philpin (Cambridge: Cambridge University Press, 1985). For differences between Sicily and Tuscany see Stephan Epstein, "Cities, Regions and the Late Medieval Crisis: Sicily and Tuscany Compared," *Past & Present,* 130 (1991): 3–50.

57. See Michael W. Dols, *The Black Death in the Middle East* (Princeton: Princeton University Press, 1977).

58. Ibid., p. 271.

59. For the beginnings of an explanation, see ibid., 293–294, and Dols, "The Comparative Communal Responses to the Black Death in Muslim and Christian Societies," *Viator,* 5 (1974): 269–287.

60. Marc Bloch, *The Historian's Craft*, trans. by Peter Putnam (Manchester: Manchester University Press, 1954 [Paris: Colin, 1949]), p. 195: "Historical facts are, in essence, psychological facts. . . . The virus of the Black Death was the prime cause of the depopulation of Europe. But the epidemic spread so rapidly only by virtue of certain social—and, therefore, in their underlying nature, mental—conditions, and its moral effects are to be explained only by the peculiar propensities of collective sensibility."

61. See John Vidal, "HIV and Risks of Ebola," *The Guardian*, May 13, 1995, p. 2, and "Science and Technology: The Hobbled Horseman," *The Economist*, May 20, 1995, pp. 79–81.

62. On Herlihy's historiography see Cohn, "David Herlihy: A Student's View," *The History Teacher*, 27, 1 (1993): 53–61; the introduction to *Portraits of Medieval and Renaissance Living: Essays in Memory of David Herlihy*, ed. by Cohn and Steven Epstein (Ann Arbor: University of Michigan Press, 1996), pp. 1–5; and Molho, "Introduction," to Herlihy, *Women, Family and Society in Medieval Europe: Historical Essays, 1978–1991* (Providence: Berghahn Books, 1995).

63. Molho, *Marriage Alliance in Late Medieval Florence* (Cambridge, Ma.: Harvard University Press, 1994), p. 2.

1. Bubonic Plague: Historical Epidemiology and the Medical Problems

1. The bibliography on the Black Death is now huge. A basic examination of medical and epidemiological character is provided by J.-N. Biraben, *Les hommes et la peste en France et dans les pays européens et méditerranéens*, 2 vols. (Paris: Mouton, 1975–76), with a large bibliography. See also Monique Lucenet, *Les grandes pestes en France* (Paris: Aubier, 1985); Robert S. Gottfried, *The Black Death: Natural and Human Disaster in Medieval Europe* (New York: Free Press, 1983).

2. The total population, city and countryside, of San Gimignano in Tuscany fell from an estimated 13,000 persons in 1332 to 3,138 in 1427—a loss of 75.9%. See David Herlihy and Christiane Klapisch-Zuber, *Les Toscans et leurs familles: Une étude du Catasto* (Paris: Foundation Nationale des Sciences Politiques, 1978), pp. 177–178

(translated as *Tuscans and Their Families: A Study of the Florentine Castato of 1427* [New Haven: Yale University Press, 1985]; they rely on Enrico Fiumi, *Storia economica e sociale di San Gimignano* (Florence: Olschki, 1961). In the countryside of Pistoia, the population declined from an estimated 37,598 persons in c. 1244 to only 8,969 in 1404—a fall of 76%. See ibid., p. 71. Bruce M. S. Campbell, "Population Pressure, Inheritance and the Land Market in a Fourteenth-Century Peasant Community," in *Land, Kinship and the Life Cycle,* ed. by Richard M. Smith (Cambridge: Cambridge University Press, 1984), pp. 87–134, concludes "that in the space of just two decades this manor's [Coltishall in Norfolk] population appears to have been reduced by 80 percent."

3. Cited in Edward O. Otis, M.D., *The Great White Plague: Tuberculosis* (New York: Crowell, 1909), p. 3.

4. Quoted in the *Boston Globe,* August 1, 1985, p. 15.

5. *Isidori Hispalensis episcopi etymologiarum sive originum libri xx,* ed. W. M. Lindsay, 2 vols. (Oxford: Clarendon, 1911), IV.6.17. "Pestilentia est contagium, quod dum unum adprehenederit, celeriter ad plures transit. . . Idem et contagium a contingendo, quia quemquem tetigerit, polluit. Ipsa et inquina, ab inquinum percussione."

6. *Oxford English Dictionary,* ed. by J. A. Simpson and E.S.C. Weiner, 2nd ed. (Oxford: Clarendon, 1989), vol. IV (under "Black Death"), p. 303, cols. 2–3.

7. *Der schwarze Tod im vierzehnten Jahrhundert. Nach den Quellen für Aerzte und gebildete Nichtarzte bearbeitet* (Berlin: Herbig, 1832).

8. *The Black Death in the Fourteenth Century,* trans. by B. G. Bagington, M.D. (London: A. Schloss, J. Wertheimer, 1833). Other editions were published in 1835, 1859, and 1885 (in New York).

9. *A History of England from the First Invasion by the Romans to the Present* (London: John Murray, 1859): "Edward's successes in France were suspended for the next six years by a pestilence, so terrible as to be called the Black Death."

10. N. H. Molaret, *Alexandre Yersin: Le vainqueur de la peste* (Paris: Fayard, 1985).

11. Indeed, contemporary chronicles commented on the possibility that animal populations may have been dislodged by earthquakes on the

eve of the Black Death. See *Manchester Medieval Source Series: The Black Death,* transl. and ed. by Rosemary Horrox (Manchester: Manchester University Press, 1994), pp. 5, 25, 34, 59, 68, 76, 83, 99, 101, 129, 161, 162, 177–182: Chronicle of Gabriele de' Mussis; Chronicle of Padua; Chronicle of the Monastery of Neuberg; Chronicle of southern Austria; Chronicle of the Abbey of Meaux; Chronicle of Henry Knighton; Chronicle of Ireland; Chronicle of Heinrich von Herford in Westphalia; Report of the Paris Medical Faculty, October 1348; and Michael W. Dols, *The Black Death in the Middle East* (Princeton, 1977), p. 39.

12. Biraben, *Les hommes et la peste,* offers the best available summary of the medical characteristics of plague.
13. The earliest chronicle of these events is Gabriele de' Mussis, *Ystoria de morbo sive mortalitate quae fuit anno Domini 1348,* in A. W. Henschel, "Document zur Geschichte des schwarzen Todes," in *Archiv für die gesammte Medicin,* ed. Heinrich Haeser (Jena, 1841), vol. II, pp. 45–57.
14. Nicephorus Gregoras, *Ecclesiasticae Historiae* in *Pathologia Graeca,* ed. Jacques-Paul Migne (Paris: Migne, 1865), vols. 148–149.
15. Francis Aidan Gasquet, *The Black Death of 1348 and 1349,* 2nd ed. (London: George Bell, 1908), in which the author surveys the plague in England, is still a useful book.
16. *Cronica di Matteo Villani* (Florence: Magheri, 1825) I, 5 (bk. I, chap. 2): "Cominciossi nelle parti d'Oriente, nel detto anno, inverso il Cattai e l'India superior, e nelle altre provincie circustanti a quelle marine dell'oceano, una pestilenzia tra gli uomini d'ogni condizione di catuna età e sesso, che cominciavane a sputare sangue, e morivano chi di subito, chi in due o in tre dì, e alquanti sostenevano più al morire. E avveniva, che chi era a servire questi malati, appicandosi quella malattia, o infetti, de quella mesesima corruzione incontanente malavano, e morivano per somigliante modo; e a' più ingrossava l'anguinaia, e a molti sotto le ditella delle bracia a destra e a sinistra, e altri in altre parti del corpo, che quasi generalmente alcuna enfiatura singulare nel corpo infetto si dimostrava."
17. See Graham Twigg, *The Black Death: A Biological Reappraisal* (London: Batsford, 1984), pp. 19–22.
18. Cited in Patrick Manson, *Tropical Diseases: A Manual of the Diseases*

of Warm Climates, rev. ed. (London: Cassell, 1903; first published in 1898), p. 242. The most recent edition, ed. by G. C. Cook, is *Manson's Tropical Diseases,* 20th ed. (London: W. B. Sanders, 1996).

19. Manson, *Tropical Diseases.*

20. Albert Camus, *La peste* (Paris: Gallimard, 1947) p. 16. After the prologue, the novel opens thus: "Le matin du 16 avril, le docteur Bernard Rieux sortit de son cabinet et buta sur un rat mort, au milieu du palier." (On the morning of April 16 Dr. Bernard Rieux walked out of his office and bumped into a dead rat in the middle of the landing.)

21. On the improbabilities of pneumonic plague, see Twigg, *The Black Death,* pp. 113ff; and Ole Jorgen Benedictow, *Plague in the Late Medieval Nordic Countries: Epidemiological Studies* (Oslo, 1992), pp. 266–267. The arguments put forward in these recent works call into question earlier claims for pneumonic plague (see for instance Christopher Morris, "The Plague in Britain," *The Historical Journal,* 14, 1 (1971), pp. 205–224).

22. Monique Lucenet, *Les grandes pestes,* p. 16.

23. Guy de Chauliac, *La grande chirurgie de Guy de Chauliac . . . composée en l'an 1363* (Paris: Alcan, 1890), vol. II, chap. 5, p. 520: "Des maladies de la poitrine et des mammelles."

24. To my reading [Cohn] it is not clear that Guy de Chauliac claimed that the second sort or wave of pestilence in 1348 was any less contagious or deadly than the first, only that in the first the victims died in three days, and in the second it took five days: "The aforesaid death began with us [in Avignon] in January [1348] and lasted seven months. It was of two sorts. The first lasted two months and was marked by continuous fever and the spitting of blood. Those afflicted died within three days. The second sort lasted for the remaining months and was also marked by continual fever and skin sores and ulcers in the intimate parts and especially in the armpits . . . And these victims died within five days. And it was greatly contagious, especially given the spitting of blood. One took the disease from another, not only through touch or breath but also through sight. As a consequence, people died without servants and were buried without priests." *The Cyrugie of Guy de Chauliac,* ed.

by Margaret S. Ogden, The Early English Text Society, no. 265 (London: Oxford University Press, 1971), p. 155 (my translation).

25. *De peste libri tres, opera Jocobi Dalechampii* (Leiden, 1552); and R. Heoniger, *Der schwarze Tod in Deutschland* (Berlin: Eugen Grosser, 1882), pp. 157–177, esp. p. 171. On Raymond, see Ernst Wickersheirmer, *Dictionnaire biographique des Médecins en France au Moyen Age* (Paris: Droz, 1936), vol. II, p. 674.] "Pestilentis morbi gravissum symptoma est, quod zonam vulgo nuncupant. Ea sic fit: Pustulae nonumquam per febres pestilentias fuscae, nigrae, lividae existunt."

26. Herlihy and Klapisch-Zuber, *Les Toscans et leurs familles,* pp. 260–262.

27. André Vauchez, *La sainteté en Occident aux derniers siècles du Moyen Age, d'après les procés de canonisation et les documents hagiographiques* (Rome: Ecole Française de Rome, 1981).

28. *Acta sanctorum quotquot toto urbe coluntur* [hereafter AS] (Paris, V. Palme, 1863).

29. AS, 2 September, p. 453.

30. Ibid. p. 456; "amorbatus eo morbo, que anguinalia dicitur."

31. Ibid. p. 453. "Anno Domini MCDLII mulier quaedam nuncupata Caterina Pauli Vannelli de Viterbo pestilentiali morbo seu fistula vexabatur in tibia, in tantum quod quasi ad mortem videbatur reducta, nec recta ulterius stare poterit . . . Mulier quaedam, Filippa Jacoba nomine, filia Angilelli, per octo annos continuos fistulas in tibia." See also further on, "Antonia . . . habens fistulam in tibia."

32. Ibid. p. 453. "Itaque omnia signa in ea mortem sibi initiari videbantur; praesertim cum per totum ejus corpus signa, quae vulgariter lenticulae cognominantur, apparuissent, in tantum, quod de ejus vita desperatum erat unicuique."

33. Ibid. p. 455. "Cum jam signa mortis in ea apparerent, quae vulgariter lenticulae cognominantur." For Petrus Dominus, see ibid., p. 456.

34. Ibid. p. 455. "Anno Domini MCLIV, cum puer quidam, annorum quatuordecim, . . . graviter infirmaretur ex pestilientiali punctura."

35. Some authorities, such as Doctor Chalmel de Viviers, who practiced in Avignon, did mention the "bubo" in 1348, but as Twigg, *The*

Black Death, p. 19, argues, buboes were not unique to *Yersinia pestis.*

36. Manson, *Tropical Diseases*, p. 250. Ecchymotic spots or patches were "few and trifling" among those infected at Hong Kong.

37. Graham Twigg, *The Black Death*. Also see his "The Black Death in England: An Epidemiological Dilemma," in *Maladies et société (XIIe-XVIIIe siècles)*, pp. 75–98.

38. Discussed in Biraben, *Les hommes et la peste*, vol. I, pp. 18–21; Lucenet, *Les grandes pestes*, p. 22, cites a source which attributes the discovery of the *Yersinia pseudotuberculosis* to Malassez and Vignal in 1893.

39. *An Essay on the Principle of Population*, ed. by Antony Flew (Harmondsworth: Penguin, 1970)

40. See especially Emmanuel Le Roy Ladurie, "L'histoire immobile," inaugural lecture given at the Collège de France, November 30, 1973, translated as "History That Stands Still," in his *The Mind and Method of the Historian*, trans. by Siân and Ben Reynolds (London: Harvester, 1981), pp. 1–27. Le Roy Ladurie interprets the entire history of Europe in terms of "long-term agrarian cycles," which are fundamentally Malthusian in character. See also his *Les paysans de Languedoc*, 2 vols. (Paris: Imprimerie Nationale, 1966).

41. Enrico Fiumi, *Storia economica*, pp. 154, 171, 174. Cited in Herlihy, *Medieval and Renaissance Pistoia: The Social History of an Italian Town* (New Haven: Yale University Press, 1967), p. 115.

42. Campbell, "Population Pressure", p. 118.

43. Cited in Lucenet, *Les grandes pestes*, p. 35.

44. *Ricordi*, ed. by V. Branca, (Florence: F. Le Monnier, 1956), p. 291.

45. Cited in Lucenet, *Les grandes pestes*, pp. 35–36.

46. Campbell, "Population Pressure," p. 128.

47. *Journal of Interdisciplinary History*, 14, 2 (1983): 199–534: "Hunger and History: The Impact of Changing Food Production and Consumption Patterns on Society"; Massimo Livi-Bacci, *Population and Nutrition: An Essay on European Demographic History*, trans. by Tania Croft-Murray (Cambridge: Cambridge University Press, 1991).

48. See Livi-Bacci, *Population and Nutrition.*

49. Campbell, "Population Pressure," p. 127.

50. Malthus's analysis was not so crude, especially in the second and later editions of *An Essay on the Principle of Population* (1798, 1803, 1806, 1807, 1817, 1826). See the recent edition and selections made by Patricia James (Cambridge: Cambridge University Press, 1992), and the discussion of Pier Paolo Viazzo, *Upland Communities: Environment, Population and Social Structure in the Alps since the Sixteenth Century* (Cambridge: Cambridge University Press, 1989), pp. 7, 42–46. See also Herlihy's own discussion of Malthus and his distinction between "positive" and "preventive" checks, below in Chapter 2.

51. "Agrarian Class Structure and Economic Development in Pre-Industrial Europe," *Past & Present,* 70 (1976):30–75. Many rejoinders from many scholars are printed in the issues following this one. See *The Brenner Debate: Agrarian Class Structure and Economic Development in Pre-Industrial Europe,* ed. by T. H. Aston and C. H. E. Philpin (Cambridge: Cambridge University Press, 1985).

52. Guy Bois, *The Crisis of Feudalism: Economy and Society in Eastern Normandy c. 1300–1550* (Cambridge: Cambridge University Press, 1984).

53. But warfare among the city-states of northern and central Italy did increase dramatically after the Black Death, and it changed fundamentally city-state finances as well as the political geography of Italy. For the wars between Florence and Milan and their fiscal consequences, see Anthony Molho, *Florentine Public Finances in the Early Renaissance, 1400–1433* (Cambridge, Mass.: Harvard University Press, 1971).

2. The New Economic and Demographic System

1. *Tutte le opere de Giovanni Boccaccio* IV: *Decameron,* ed. by Vittore Branca (Milan: Mondador, 1976), "Giornata I, Introduzione," p. 13.

2. Ibid. p. 18.

3. *Jugement du Roi de Navarre,* cited in Lucenet, *Les grandes pestes,* p. 45.

4. *Decameron,* "Giornata I, Introduzione," p. 16.

5. Ibid. p. 11.
6. Cited in Gasquet, *The Black Death of 1348 and 1349*, 2nd ed. (London: George Bell, 1908), pp. 81–82. [The original comes from D. Wilkins, *Concilia Magnae Britanniae et Hiberniae*, 4 vols. (London: R. Gosling, 1737), vol. II, p. 738, which Herlihy appears to have consulted for his translation; it differs markedly from Gasquet's.]
7. See Mario Ascheri, *Diritto e peste: Dalla crisi del Trecento all'età moderna* (Siena, 1974); and Paolo Zacchia, *Quaestiones medicolegales* (Leipzig [lipsiae], 1630).
8. Herlihy, "The Generation in European History," in *The Social History of Italy and Western Europe* (London: Variorum reprints, 1978), no. 12, p. 351, puts the results of J. C. Russell's examination of the longevity of members of the English royal family together with data about the lives of contemporary Florentine merchants.
9. Herlihy and Klapisch-Zuber, *Les Toscans et leurs familles*, pp. 370–389.
10. See Herlihy, "Generation," p. 355. The figures are based on the years between profession and death passed by the Dominicans of Santa Maria Novella in Florence.
11. Archivio di Stato de Firenze (henceforth, ASF), Manoscritti, reg. 943, a compilation made in the seventeenth century.
12. On the contemporary life of the Florentine reformer Fra Giovanni Dominici, see *Acta Sanctorum*, 2 June (Antwerp, 1698), p. 407. On di Caroli, see Salvatore Camporeale, "Giovanni Caroli e la 'Vitae fratrum S. M. Novellai': Umanesimo e crisi religiosa (1460–1480)," *Memorie Domenicane*, n.s., 16 (1985): 199–233; his "Humanism and the Religious Crisis of the late Quattrocento: Giovanni Caroli O.P., and the 'Liber dierum lucensium," in *Christianity and the Renaissance: Image and Religious Imagination in the Quattrocento*, ed. by Timothy Verdon and John Henderson (Syracuse, N.Y., 1990), pp. 445–66; and his "Giovanni Caroli, 1460–1480: Death, Memory and Transformation," in *Life and Death in Fifteenth-Century Florence*, ed. by M. Tetel, R. Witt and R. Goffen (Durham, N.C.: Duke University Press, 1989), pp. 16–27.
13. *Cronica di Matteo Villani*, ed. I. Moutier (Florence: Magheri,

1825), p. 11 (bk. I, chap. 5): "Stimossi per il mancamento della gente dovere essere dovizia di tutte le cose che la terra produce, e in contradio per l'ingratitudine degli uomini ogni cosa venne in disusata carestia, e continovò lungo tempo: ma in certi paesi, come nararemo, furono gravi e disusate fami. E ancora si pensò essere dovizia e abbondanza di vestimenti, e di tutte l'altre cose che al corpo umano sono di bisogno oltre alla vita, e il contrario apparve in fatto lungamente; che due cotanti o più volsono le maggior parte delle cose che valere non soleano innanzi alla detta mortalità. E il lavorio, e le manifatture d'ogni arte a mestiero montò oltre al doppio consueto disordinatamente."

14. Literature cited in Charles M. de la Roncière, *Florence: Centre economique regional au XIVe siècle* (Aix-en-Provence: S.O.D.E.B., 1976), vol. II, p. 772.

15. Richard Goldthwaite, "I prezzi del grano a Firenze dal XIV al XVI secolo," *Quaderni Storici,* 28 (1975): 5–36.

16. *Cronica di Matteo Villani,* I, 10 (bk. I, chap. 4).

17. Ibid., I, 93. Cited from the original matriculation lists.

18. On Gutenberg and the technology of early printing see Victor Scholderer, *Johann Gutenberg: The Inventor of Printing* (London, 1963); D. C. McMurtrie, *The Invention of Printing* (Chicago, 1942); and Janet T. Ing, *Johann Gutenberg and His Bible: A Historical Study* (New York: The Typophile, 1988).

19. Ibn Khaldun, *The Muqaddimah: An Introduction to History,* 3 vols., transl. by Franz Rosenthal, 2nd ed. (Princeton: Princeton University Press, 1967); *Quinti Septimii Florentis Tertullianim Opera omnia in Patrilogia latina,* vols. 1–2, ed. by Jacques-Paul Migne (Paris: Migne, 1978–79); Niccolò Machiavelli, *Opere,* ed. by Mario Bonfantini (Milan: Ricciardi, 1954).

20. See Donald Winch's introduction to Malthus's *An Essay on the Principle of Population* (Cambridge: Cambridge University Press, 1992), pp. xiv–xv. In the second and subsequent editions, as Malthus gathered more empirical data from places such as Norway and the mountains of Switzerland, he also began to view these "preventive checks" as better than simple vices, classifying delayed marriage and celibacy as "moral constraints."

21. E. A. Wrigley and R. Schofield, *The Population History of England*

1541–1871: A Reconstruction (London: Edward Arnold, 1981). See also E. A. Wrigley, "The Growth of Population in Eighteenth-Century England: A Conundrum Resolved," *Past & Present*, 98 (1983): 121–150.

22. *Polyptyque de l'abbaye de Saint-Germain des Près*, ed. by Auguste Longnon (Paris: H. Champion, 1886).

23. In calculating the following averages, we do not specify the different units by which plowlands and vineyards and meadows are measured. They are simply added together. Undifferentiated groups of persons in a household not otherwise identified by number or sex (chiefly children) are counted as two persons. The treatment of the data is admittedly robust, but even if attempts at refinement are made, the association between land size and household size remains very strong.

24. On the poor in medieval society, see Michel Mollat, *Les pauvres au Moyen Age, étude sociale*, 2nd ed. (Paris: Hachette, 1978).

25. For a criticism of this analysis, see Diane O. Hughes, "From Brideprice to Dowry in Mediterranean Europe," *Journal of Family History*, 3 (1978): 262–296, especially p. 285. Herlihy first suggested this interpretation in "The Generation in Medieval History," *Viator*, 5 (1974): 347–364.

26. See Herlihy, *Medieval Households* (Cambridge, Mass.: Harvard University Press, 1985), pp. 67–68.

27. Giovanni Villani, *Cronica* (Florence, 1833), V, 212, (bk. 10, chap. 162): "A tutti i poveri di Firenze, i quali andassone per limonsine, fossono dati denari sei per uno."

28. *Cronica di Matteo Villani*, I, 7 (p. 13): "E i mendichi poveri erano quasi tutti morti, e ogni femminella era piena e abbondevole delle cose."

29. Ibid. p. 14: "E non essendo in quel tempo poveri bisognosi."

30. Alessandro Righi, *Historia contagiosi morbi, qui Florentiam populatus fuit anno 1630* (Florence: Typis Francisci Honufrii, 1633), 26–27, rub. 7. "Super pauperes et egenos tantum. Quoniam autem pauperes, et egeni sunt totius Civitatis pars ignobilior, et debilior, nec possunt molestias ad alios transmictere, ideo necessario, siquid mali in Civitate est, ipsi recipiunt, & retinent, cum sint glandulae Civitatis, sicut glandulae sunt pauperes corporis, sed animi etiam magis, faciliusque quam alii homines recipiunt; sunt autem animi

morbi ipsa vitia." Cited in Giulia Calvi, *Storia di un anno di peste: Comportamenti sociali e immaginario nella Firenze barocca* (Milan: Bompiani, 1984), p. 76.
31. Herlihy and Klapisch-Zuber, *Les Toscans et leurs familles*, pp. 476–479.

3. Modes of Thought and Feeling

1. *Decameron,* "Giornata I, Introduzione," p. 15. On psychological reactions to the plague, see the extensive discussion by Jean Delumeau, *La peur en Occident (XIVe-XVIIIe siècles): Une cité assiegée* (Paris: Fayard, 1978), pp. 98–142, on "Typologie de comportements collectifs en temps de peste." On funerals during the Renaissance, see Sharon T. Strocchia, *Death and Ritual in Renaissance Florence* (Baltimore: Johns Hopkins University Press, 1992).
2. Jacques Chiffoleau, *La comptabilité de l'au-delà: Les hommes, la mort et la religion dans la region d'Avignon à la fin du Moyen Age (vers 1320-vers 1480).* Collection de l'Ecole Française de Rome, 47 (Rome: Ecole Française, 1980), pp. 126–149.
3. Jean de Venette, *Chronique Latine de Guillaume de Nangis, avec les continuations de cette chronique,* ed. by H. Geraud (Paris: J. Renouard, 1843), vol. II, pp. 210–216, cited in *Manchester Medieval Source Series: The Black Death,* transl. and ed. by Rosemary Horrox (Manchester: Manchester University Press, 1994), p. 55.
4. *Decameron,* "Giornata I, Introduzione," pp. 15–16.
5. Letter of Louis Sanctus de Beeringen, ed. de Smet, *Recueil des Chroniques de Flandre* (Brusells, 1956), vol. III, p. 17, cited in Chiffoleau, *Comptabilité,* pp. 203–204.
6. Giulia Calvi, *Storia di un anno di peste. Comportamenti sociali e immaginario nella Firenze barocca* (Milan: Bompiani, 1984), makes much use of the records of the Florentine Sanità during the plague of 1630 and gives many examples of prosecutions arising out of the failure to report family members sick of the plague.
7. See Alberto Tenenti, *Il senso della morte e l'amore della via nel Rinascimento (Francia e Italia)* (Turin: Einaudi, 1957); Philippe Ariès, *Western Attitudes toward Death: From the Middle Ages to the Present,* transl. by P. Ranum (Baltimore: Johns Hopkins University Press, 1974) and his *The Hour of Our Death,* transl. by Helen

Weaver (New York: Vintage Books, 1977). Also see the comments of Salvatore Camporeale, "Senso della morte e amore della vita nel Rinascimento: Susone, Valla, Erasmo, e il 'problema della salvezza,' " *Memorie Domenicane*, n.s. 8–9 (1977–78): 439–450.

8. A. McGee Morganstern, "The La Grange Tomb and Choir; A Monument of the Great Schism in the West," *Speculum*, 48 (1973): 52–69.

9. Cited in Chiffoleau, *Comptabilité*, frontispiece.

10. See Ariès, *Western Attitudes toward Death*, ch. 1.

11. *Decameron*, "Giornata I, Introduzione," p. 16.

12. On the cemeteries of Avignon and the acts perpetrated in them, see Chiffoleau, *Comptabilité*, pp. 154–165.

13. *Decameron*, "Giornata I, Introduzione," p. 13.

14. *Cronica di Matteo Villani*, I, chap. 4 (I, pp. 10–11).

15. Ibid., I, chap. 56 (I, pp. 90–91).

16. *The Canterbury Tales*, modern English by Frank E. Hill (New York, 1960), pp. 11, 17–18.

17. Herlihy does not make clear the source for these numbers. Instead of a decline, William J. Courtenay, "The Effect of the Black Death on English Higher Education," *Speculum*, 55, 4 (1980): 696–714, finds a rise in the numbers enrolled at Oxford after the Black Death; from 1,086 (1340–1359) to 1,547 (1380–1399). Courtenay's source is *The Biographical Register of the University of Oxford* computerized under the direction of T. H. Aston. See also Aston, "Oxford's Medieval Alumni," *Past & Present*, 74 (1977): 3–40.

18. While Herlihy's reading of Galen would have been the standard one still by the mid-1980s, medical historians have since shown that a theory of contagion was neither foreign to Galen nor to those who had been trained in the Galenic traditions of the Middle Ages, that is, doctors such as Guy de Chauliac; see Jon Arrizabalaga, "Facing the Black Death: Perceptions and Reactions of University Medical Practitioners," in *Practical Medicine from Salerno to the Black Death*, ed. by L. García-Ballester, R. French, J. Arrizabalaga, and A. Cunningham (Cambridge: Cambridge University Press, 1994), pp. 237–288; and Vivian Nutton, "The Seeds of Disease: An Explanation of Contagion and Infection from the Greeks to the Renaissance," *Medical History*, 27 (1983), 1–34.

19. Medical historians have recently attributed less significance to Fra-

castoro's theories of contagion and do not consider them a radical departure from the supposed miasmic theories of Galen and his late medieval scholastic followers; see previous note.

20. J. Delumeau, *Le catholicisme entre Luther et Voltaire* (Paris: Presses Universitaires de France, 1971).

21. "La chretienté vers 1500 c'est, presque, un pays du mission," cited in John Van Engen, "The Christian Middle Ages as an Historiographical Problem," *American Historical Review,* 91 (1986): 519–552. See Jacques Le Goff, *La civilisation de l'occident médiéval* (Paris: Arthaud, 1964), pp. 18–19.

22. *Polyptyque de l'abbaye de Saint-Germain des Près,* ed. by Auguste Longnon, 2 vols. (Paris: H. Champion, 1886).

23. Olof Brattö, *Studi di antroponimia fiorentina: Il libro de Montaperti* (Goteborg, 1953); and his *Nuovi studi di antroponimia fiorentina: I nomi meno frequenti del Libro di Montaperti (An. MCCLX)* in *Acta Universitatis Gothoburgensis,* vol. 61 (Stockholm: Almquist and Wiksell, 1955).

24. See ranking of names for the city and contado of Florence, 1260, by Brattö, *Antroponimia,* p. 34.

25. In the countryside, Iacobus and Iohannes trade position. See the distribution given in ibid.

26. Stefano Orlandi, O.P., *"Necrologio" di S. Maria Novella,* 2 vols. (Florence: L. S. Olschki, 1955).

27. Among officials elected at Florence between 1451 and 1500, Francesco appears 4,105 times, and Giovanni 4,090. After 1500, it scores 724 as compared to 692 for Giovanni.

28. On saints as defenders against disease, see the recent comprehensive survey by C. L. Trub, *Heilige und Krankheit, Geschichte und Gesellschaft,* Bochumer Historische Studien, 19 (Stuttgart: Klett-Cotta, 1978), pp. 48–53 and Table 4, pp. 252–253, in which he names 60 saints, 50 men and ten women (11 percent of 547 medical saints he identifies) as patrons against the plague.

29. S. Bernadino da Siena: *Opera omnia,* ed. PP. Collegii S. Bonaventurae (Florence: Colegii S. Bonaventurae, 1950): "Nam quibusdam sanctis divinitus datus est in alicuibus causis praecipue patrocinari, sicut sancto Antonio de Padua ordinis Minorum quotidie eius petrociniis gratias et miracula impetrara."

30. Among Florentine officials the name appears 97 times. (This evi-

dence comes from Herlihy's work on the Tratte and his last major research project, which was cut short by his death. It was the prosopography of the Florentine ruling class from the Black Death to the fall of the Republic in 1530. Herlihy completed two pilot studies for this project: "Age, Property and Career in Medieval Society," in *Aging and the Aged in Medieval Europe,* ed. by M. M. Sheehan, CSB Papers in Medieval Studies, 11 (Toronto: Pontifical Institute of Medieval Studies, 1990), pp. 143–158; and "The Rulers of Florence, 1282–1530," in *Athens and Rome, Florence and Venice: City-States in Classical Antiquity and Medieval Italy,* ed. by Anthony Molho, Kurt Raaflaub, and Julia Emlen (Stuttgart: Steiner, 1991), pp. 197–221 (both reprinted in *Women, Family and Society in Medieval Europe: Historical Essays, 1978–1991,* ed. by Anthony Molho [Providence: Berghahn Books, 1995]).

31. See Francesco Diedo's legend of St. Rosa da Viterbo in *Acta Sanctorum* [hereafter AS], September 2 (Antwerp, 1748); and Fausta Casolini, "Rosa da Viterbo," in *Bibliotheca Sanctorum: Istituto Giovanni XXIII della Pontifica Università Lateranense* [hereafter BS] (Rome, Istituto Giovanni XXIII, 1968), vol. XI, pp. 414–425.

32. See Agostino Amore, "Rosalia di Palermo, santa," 1160 BS, XI, pp. 427–433; AS (Venice, 1756), pp. 278–414.

33. On Domenica da Paradiso, venerabile (1473–1553), see Sadoc M. Bertucci, BS, IV, pp. 678–680 (1964); and S. Razzi, *Vite dei Santi e Beati Toscani* (Florence, 1601), vol. II, p. 100.

34. André Vauchez, "Rocco, santo," BS, XI, pp. 264–73; and AS (Anversa, 1737), pp. 407–410; F. Diedo, *Vita Sancti Rochi (1479),* ibid., pp. 400–407.

35. Chiffoleau, *Comptabilité.*

36. In view of the history of anti-Semitism and other racist ideologies, some may wish to question Herlihy's optimistic conclusion. Of course, the debate among modern and contemporary historians and political scientists is still open on whether the rebirth of these sentiments in the nineteenth century can be linked with the post-Black Death spree of Jewish pogroms and attacks on foreigners.

Index

Index

British Library, 85n, 93n
Bulst, Neithard, 85n, 86n, 89n
bureaucracy, *see* government
burial, 60–62; *see also* cemeteries,
    funerals, tombs
Bynum, Caroline, 90n

Cairo, 24
Calais, 25
Calvi, Giulia, 107n
Cambridge (University), 69–70
Campbell, Bruce, 4, 12, 14, 33–34,
    85n, 95n, 98n, 102n
Camporeale, Salvatore, 92n, 104n,
    108n
Camus, Albert, 26, 100n
Canterbury Tales, *see* Chaucer
Canton, 26
capital, 49
Carmichael, Ann, 86n, 89n, 90n
Carolingian capitularies, 55
Carus-Wilson, Eleanora, 94n
Catasto of 1427, *see* Florence
celestial conjunctures, 3
cemeteries, 23, 64, 66; *see also* burials
Chalmel de Viviers (doctor), 101n
Chambéry (France), 65
charity, 55; *see also* piety
Charles IV, Emperor, 70
Chaucer, Geoffrey, 67, 108n
Chiffoleau, Jacques, 107n, 108n,
    110n
children, 9–10, 34, 43–44, 47, 57, 69,
    73
China, 20–23, 26, 52
Chinon (Lake Geneva), 65
cholera, 4–5, 19, 87n, 88n, 89n
Christianity, 8, 73–74; *see also* names,
    theology
Christopher, St., 78
church, 60
Cipolla, Carlo, 95n
class (social), 4–5, 35, 27; middle class,
    56

Clement VI, Pope, 7, 65, 67–68
clergy, 45–46, 69; *see also* mendicants,
    priests
climate, 26–27, 30
clothing, 48; *see also* technology:
    textiles
Cohn, Samuel, 93n, 96n, 97n
Cologna, 25
Coltishall (Norfolk), 4, 33, 98n
Colyton (Devon), 92n
commerce, trade, 23
comparative history, 13
Constantinople, 24
contagion, 10
Copenhagen, 25
corpse, *see* body
Cosmas and Damian, Saints, 79
Council of Constance, 80
Courtenay, William, 88n, 108n
Cracow, 70
craftsmen, 44; *see also* professions
Crosby, Alfred, 87n

Danish chroniclers, 19
Dauphiné, Province of (France), 68
death, 60; image of 63–64; *see also*
    plague: mortality figures; population
Decameron, see Boccaccio
de Chauliac, Guy, 7, 27, 65, 91n,
    100n, 108n
Delumeau, Jean, 73, 109n
demography, *see* population, systems of
    behavior
de Mussis, Gabrielle, 9, 99n
dependency ratios, 44
de Venette, Jean, 107n
Diedo, Francesco, 80, 110n
Dini, Bruno, 94n
doctors (medicine), *see* physicians
Dohar, William, 88n
Dols, Michael, 14, 96n
Domenica da Paridiso, S., 79, 110n
Dominicans, 77; *see also* mendicants,
    Santa Maria Novella

Index

Herlihy, David, 1–15, 83n–84n, 87n, 92n–97n, 101n, 103n, 104n, 106n–109n; historiography of, 1–2
Hong Kong, 20–21
Horrox, Rosemary, 86n, 90n, 92n, 93n, 99n
hospitals, 62
households, 53–54, 56
Hughes, Diane, 106n
Huizinga, Johan, 8, 92n

Iacopo di Campostella, St., 75
Ibn Khaldun, 105n
Ile–de–France, 47
incunabula, 11, 93n
India, 21–22, 26
industrial revolution, 10–11, 53
inflation, *see* prices
influenza, 89n, 90n
Ing, Janet, 105n
inheritance, 65
Ireland, 25; potato blight (1847), 33, 53
Isidore of Seville, 98n
Issyk Kul, 23
Italy, 10, 20, 24, 67–68, 89n

Jenks, Stuart, 90n
Jews, 59, 64–66; *see also* anti-Semitism
John, St., 75
Judea, 24

Kaffa, 24–25
Khvolson (Soviet archeologist), 23
Kiev, 25
Klapisch–Zuber, Christiane, 92n, 97n, 101n, 104n, 107n

labor, 48–50, 52, 57
la Grange, Cardinal of Avignon, 63
land, 49, 54
Langland, William, 9, 88n, 93n
languages, 71

Languedoc, 32
la Roncière, Charles Marie de, 12, 96n, 105n
Latin, 71
law, 42; canon, 64; sumptuary, 48; Roman, 54, 64
Le Goff, Jacques, 73, 109n
Leoni, Francesco, 89n
lepers, 59, 64
Le Roy Ladurie, Emmanuel, 2, 31, 84n, 102n
Libri dei morti (Florence), 27
Libro di Montaperti, 12, 75
life expectancies, 43
Livi–Bacci, Massimo, 4, 85n, 102n
Lonni, Ada, 87n–88n
Lorenzo, S., 78
Lübeck, 25
Lucenet, Monique, 97n, 100n, 102n, 103n
lust, 65
Lybia, 24

Macedonia, 24
Machiavelli, Niccolò, 105n
Mainz, 50
malnutrition, 4, 33–34, 52; *see also* famine
Malthus, Thomas; Malthusian approach, 2–4, 8, 31–35, 37–39, 46, 51–53, 81, 102n, 103n
Mamluks, 13
Manson, Patrick, 99n–100n, 102n
Marco Polo, 23
marginals, 59, 66
marriage, 52, 54–55, 57
Marseilles, 24
Martin of Tours, St., 74
Marx, Karl; Marxist analysis, 4, 31, 34–35
Mary, the Virgin, 80
mass, 80
McMurtrie, D. C., 105n
Medici (family), 79

Index